Sufi Sage of Arabia

Imām

ᶜAbdallāh al-Ḥaddād

Sufi Sage of Arabia

By

MOṢṬAFĀ AL-BADAWĪ

FONS VITAE

First published in 2005 by
Fons Vitae
49 Mockingbird Valley Drive
Louisville, KY 40207
http://www.fonsvitae.com
Email: fonsvitaeky@aol.com

Library of Congress Control Number: 2004118252

ISBN 1-887752-65-X

Gratitude for the use of their photography goes to Isma'il Pennino (for the cover photograph), Sayyid 'Alawi Bilfaqih, Sayyid Muhammad al-Haddad, Sayyid Mustafa al-Mehdar, 'Umar Bajkhayf, and Ibrahim Izzat Pasha.

With special thanks to Sarah Yost for her work in editing.

This book was typeset by Neville Blakemore, Jr.

Printed in Canada

CONTENTS

Two paths to God exist for the people of this world, the path of salvation and the path of sanctification. For those who seek more than the minimum, who desire more than the average man, who want and yearn for intimate knowledge of their source and ultimate destiny, sanctification allows them that possibility. The Prophets are sanctified souls that are specially prepared by their Lord, not only as a vessel of divine knowledge but also as the means of conveying it to others. For the men and women who take from them and come after them heeding their call, it is through the path of sanctification that the prophetic path is continued in this world for others to walk the path of salvation. Without sanctified souls in the world, the path would eventually be lost, and those seeking salvation destroyed. For those who the saints call, sanctification is a process that continues throughout one's life on earth and is finalized with a purified soul that is content and ready to return to God in a sanctified state. These souls are then able to act as milestones for those on the path of salvation. They inspire us and direct us to strive on and keep the goal of God's presence in our hearts. Imām al-Haddād was such a soul. He, through his own teachers, tended to his soul and journeyed on the path of sanctification in order to realize the true alchemy of the hearts, turning the self from a base element, susceptible to corruption, into pure spiritual gold, free of the corrosive elements of this world.

This book, while a biography of one of the greatest saints in Islamic history, is more than that. It is a book of alchemy itself, filled from start to finish with the science of *tasawwuf*, which is and has always been the heart of the Islamic tradition. It was written by a practitioner of the outward science of psychology and the inward science of the *nafs* or soul, which, in the path of salvation, works to confine itself to the laws of the sacred order as articulated by the prophets, and, in Islam's case, by the last and final messenger, Muhammad (peace be upon him), and, in the path of sanctification, works to move through the well-established states and stations of the wayfarer until true knowledge of God is realized.

Dr. Badawī was a student of a direct descendant of Shaykh 'Abdallah al-Haddād, Habīb Ahmad Mashshūr al-Haddīd, who those of us fortunate enough to have known him personally consider a realized spiritual master and sanctified soul, and none can sanctify save God. Habīb Ahmad Mashshūr was an antidote for the insanity that accompanies so much religious imbalance in our times. Just as his ancestor, the subject of this book, brought renewal and light to the Islam of his time, today's masters maintain that same light in a time that might be referred to as the endarkenment. This book is a compelling testimony to the spiritual power and influence of the sanctified soul on the world. It is, perhaps more importantly for us, a step toward reintroducing the desperately needed path of sanctification. If there was ever a time that saints were needed, it is this time.

Shaykh Hamza Yusuf

Preface

Today, almost three centuries after Imām ᶜAbdallāh ibn ᶜAlawī al-Ḥaddād's death in 1720, it is not difficult to see why his influence seems to be growing more powerful by the day and his knowledge continues to spread far and wide. Because he was one of the most accomplished scholars of all time, as well as a giant of Muslim spirituality, the task of renewing Islam fell upon him. His work restates traditional Islamic knowledge in the form best suited for his time and succeeding centuries, and has also modified the spiritual methodology of the Sufis, rendering it suitable for the Muslims of the "End of Time." This modified practice he called the "Method of the Companions of the Right Hand," in order to distinguish it from the much stricter "Method of the Drawn Near" of his ancestors and other previous Sufis. In all these endeavors the Imām always represented the strictest orthodox current within Islam.

Imām al-Ḥaddād received two divine gifts that were perceptible even to ordinary Muslims. The first was his ability to accurately read the developments that were to ail the Islamic community, rendering most Muslims incapable of either perusing or understanding the masterpieces of the great Imāms of old. The second was the ability to express profound truths in a brief, yet astoundingly clear way. The combination of these gifts has made his writings among the most practically useful sources for the Muslims of our time in terms of a theoretical understanding of traditional Islam in all its wisdom, while remaining an easily followed guide for its application.

Imām al-Ḥaddād is still present in the lives of many Muslims. The anniversary of his death continues to be commemorated each year on all five continents. His *awrād* are recited daily by thousands of Muslims. His poems, which radiate love, wisdom, and knowledge, are among the most frequently sung verses in spiritual gatherings. His books have been and still are being reprinted almost yearly, formerly in Cairo but now more often in Beirut and Singapore. Many of his works have been translated into a number of languages and are benefiting thousands of people everywhere. His spiritual method is still being implemented by ᶜAlawī masters, producing more masters, and thereby continually proving its efficacy in assisting spiritual travelers along the path to fruition.

The relevance of this biography is therefore manifold. Since the Imām's works are being studied by so many thousands of English speakers, many of them will naturally wish to know more about the author. This inquiry will undoubtedly lead to a stronger emotional attachment to him, and therefore to a greater effulgence of *baraka*, and thus engender a greater capacity to benefit from his writings. Others, perhaps attracted to Sufism though undecided as to its merits, will find much benefit from studying the life of a spiritual leader of such magnitude. Still others, harboring false ideas about the Sufi path prevalent among superficially educated Muslims of today, may find it interesting to learn about the inward spiritual dimension of so great an exoteric scholar. Over the years, many of the eminent scholars of the Muslim community have been spiritual men, whether they permit their spirituality to shine outwardly or not. As for non-Muslims, I hope they will find here much of the real worth of Islam and its most profound meaning.

No biography can ever do justice to men of this caliber and versatility. One should note that the Imām often kept his inner states hidden. What he allowed to be noticed outwardly were the few glimpses that he felt were necessary to reveal in order to best carry out his various functions. Similarly, the Imām could not entrust much of his inward knowledge to the pages of a book as this might invite misinterpretation. The little we do have is nevertheless of immense value, as shall become clear to the reader.

I was told by a friend in the publishing business that for the Western reader such a description of the Imām's life might seem to be an idealization, even leaving aside the few supernatural events I mention. There is little that can be done about that since the very concept of sanctity has become incomprehensible to the modern mentality. However, near perfect people do exist, and not just as legends. I have met many men of God whose character and behavior bore witness that such great saints as the Imām are still alive among Muslims today. Many people I know have also personally witnessed such a number of supernatural events as to render them ordinary, everyday occurrences, far from hearsay.

There were three main sources for this biography, the first of which was the Imām's major Arabic biography, written shortly after his death by one of his closest disciples, Imām Muḥammad ibn Sumayṭ, and published in Cairo in 1990 C.E. The second source was the book of Shaykh Aḥmad al-Shajjār, who collected all he was able to note of the Imām's utterances over the course of sixteen years. These were recorded in the work, *Tathbīt al-Fu'ād,* printed in Cairo in 1981 C.E. and again in Singapore in 1999 C.E. The third important source was the two-volume collection of his correspondence, edited by Imām Aḥmad ibn Zayn al-Ḥabashī, and printed in Cairo in 1979 C.E. Other sources include information gleaned from the Imām's descendants (received by oral transmission from their forefathers), his published works, and his *Dīwān* of poetry.

We hope that by making this exceptional scholar and saint better known to the public, we will have contributed to the dissemination of his message to the community, which was always the Imām's dearest wish.

Success comes from none other than God, may He be praised and thanked for what He has granted.

Imām
ᶜAbdallāh al-Ḥaddād

Sufi Sage of Arabia

Chapter 1
TARĪM

The descendants of the Prophet reach South Yemen—spread of the Sunni Shāfiᶜī school—civil strife in Hadramawt—Tarīm becomes the capital of the Sayyids—the Ḥaddād clan acquire their name—birth of the Imām.

In the fourth century of the *Hijra* (tenth century C.E.), Imām Aḥmad ibn ᶜĪsā decided to emigrate from the troubled land of Iraq. He was the descendant of Imām Jaᶜfar al-Ṣādiq and was thus a Ḥusaynī *sharīf* endowed with the breadth and depth of knowledge that is the prerogative of the House about which the Prophet had said: "The likeness of the People of my House amongst you is that of Noah's Ark, those who came on board were saved and those who failed to do so perished."[1]

For just as Noah's ark was, for his people, the divinely ordained, and therefore the only effective means of salvation from the flood, the descendants of the Prophet, may God's blessings and peace be upon him and his family, remain the divinely ordained means of salvation for his community by being the repositories of Qur'ānic knowledge. This truth was declared unequivocally by the Prophet, may God's blessings and peace be upon him and his family, when he stated publicly that he had bequeathed for his community two things to hold on to so as never to stray: The Qur'ān and the People of House. He further assured them that the two were never to part company until the time they rejoin him at the Pool in the course of the events following the Resurrection.[2] The implication here is that the many dimensions of meaning in the Qur'ān, the art of interpretation, and the method necessary to convert theory into practice so as to reach the goal, are to be found eminently in the leaders among the People of the House. To attach oneself to them and to follow their example is a means of sailing through the tumultuous waters of temptation, seditions, discords, and other perils that are inevitably to befall mankind and spread as time goes by. This is not to say that knowledge is restricted to the direct descendants of the Prophet, may God's blessings and peace be upon him and his family, for his community has produced innumerable great scholars and men of God in all races. People of the House remain, however, the principal repository of the highest kind of Qur'ānic knowledge, a fact attested to by history and more importantly, by orthodox scholars and men of God.

Imām Aḥmad ibn ᶜĪsā (later known as al-Muhājir) the Emigrant, headed South towards Madina where he spent a year, following which he headed for Makka, performed *ḥajj*, and then resumed his journey which ended in the valley of Hadramawt. His descendants became known as the Children of ᶜAlawī, Banū-ᶜAlawī or Bā-ᶜAlawī in Hadramī parlance; ᶜAlawī was Imām Aḥmad's grandson and the ancestor of all ᶜAlawī *sayyids.* Their main base became Tarīm, while some lived in neighbouring towns such as Shibām, Sayūn, and Qaydūn, all located inland. A lesser number settled in the coastal towns of al-Shiḥr, al-Mukallā, and Aden. They were Sunnis in their beliefs and had adopted the Shāfiᶜī school of jurisprudence, since Imām al-Shāfiᶜī was, according to Imām al-Ḥaddād, "the master of the independent (*Mujtahid*) Imāms, after the Companions and the Followers."

Tarīm

Mausoleum of Imām Aḥmad ibn ᶜĪsā, the first of the descendants of the Prophet to emigrate to Hadramawt and the ancestor of all Bā-ᶜAlawī *sayyids*. The grave at the bottom of the hill is that of Sayyid Aḥmad al-Ḥabashī, Imām Ḥaddād's maternal great-grandfather.

The secret of the House of Prophecy thus manifested itself in the valley of Hadramawt, appearing with great force in succeeding generations of superb scholars, great saints, spiritual masters, and summoners to the One and to the Muḥammadan way. From there this radiated to the east and the west, carrying Islam in its purest form to South-East Asia, parts of India, and the East African coast. The people of these lands have remained to this day in the ᶜAlawī tradition, Sunnis and Shāfiᶜīs, with a strong inclination towards Sufism.

Hadramawt was not blessed with water or other vital resources; it is an austere land whose inhabitants know nothing of the comforts and luxuries of more affluent countries, and remain totally dependent on rainfall for their meagre crops. Islam was originally carried to the south of the Arabian Peninsula by the Companions of the Prophet. This land was never at peace for very long. The tribesmen were given to internecine strife, as each tribe would make a bid for supremacy whenever they perceived a chance for success, only to be opposed by the others in various ephemeral coalitions. The Zaydīs of North Yemen, a Shīᶜa sect, made numerous incursions into Hadramawt, and during the lifetime of Imām al-Ḥaddād, they effectively gained sovereignty over much of it. They invaded Hadramawt in 1070 A.H., ruling until ousted by the Yāfeᶜīs, the hardy tribesmen of the Yāfeᶜ mountainous region to the west, in 1117 A.H. During these forty-seven years, the *adhān* was called from the minarets of Shāfiᶜī Hadramawt in the Zaydī manner, with the exception of the *muazzin* of the Bā-ᶜAlawī mosque, who stubbornly refused to comply despite repeated threats.

Long before the Zaydī invasion of 1070 A.H. the Kathīrī clan had established relative political supremacy. They became the sultans of the land, sometimes quarrelling amongst themselves and dividing the land into multiple sultanates. It was one of these quarrels that gave the Zaydīs the pretext to invade. The Kathīrīs remained in power during and subsequent to both the Zaydī and Yāfe^{c}ī periods, and there are several letters from Imām al-Ḥaddād to them preserved in his published correspondence.

The Yāfe^{c}ī period was one of sufferings and trials for the population. There were battles between the Yāfe^{c}īs and the Kathīrī sultans, many ending in stalemate followed by reprisals. The ^{c}Alawīs always kept aloof from such events, only intervening in the form of counsels given to the sultans and other officials. Later another clan, the Qu^{c}aytīs, overtook part of the land and remained the sultans of al-Mukallā until modern times.

Most of the ^{c}Alawīs are buried in the great cemetery of Tarīm, the Bashshār cemetery. There is a special area reserved for them called Zanbal. For this reason the ^{c}Alawīs refer to the cemetery sometimes as Bashshār and sometimes as Zanbal in their writings and poems.

Such was the influence of the ^{c}Alawī scholars that everyone in the city was bred into behaving in a pattern thoroughly conforming with *sharī^{c}a*, so that every transaction, whether in the marketplace or elsewhere, was carried out in the correct manner. Even those who did not know learned unconsciously by simply being there. Thus, Tarīm was said to be "the teacher of he who has no teacher."

Despite the political turbulence, the people at this time were much closer to *sharī^{c}a* than they are today, which was because the environment forced them into an almost ascetic mode of living. Yet their practices were still so remote from the ideal Islamic society in the Imām's mind that he often complained about the rarity of those who were seriously interested in their religion. Temptations and makers of seditions were, to his mind, too many. The people's hearts were divided because they were obsessed with the accumulation of worldly things. Many of the inhabitants of Tarīm, he once remarked, were unaware of the existence of his books. In one of his letters he writes: "The people of the time, as you can see, are people of sedition and discord, wasteful of one another's rights and transgressing beyond limits. Were someone to govern them who neither resembles nor suits them, he would find himself in trouble and things would take a critical turn for both him and them. The righteous man is as precious as a jewel, and the people of this time are like those who are holding dirty stones with which to either break or soil it." In another letter he says: "This is a time when honesty has gone, religion has grown weak, and treachery has become rampant. The people are in chaos, their energies are concentrated in their stomachs and genitals; it is equal to them whether they are falling or rising, and so long as they obtain their worldly desires, they care nothing for how they fare with their Lord."

In a different vein, however, he once remarked, "Tarīm is the town of the *sayyids* and the superior people. To live therein is a gain for the virtuous and the righteous. There is nothing to match it nowadays except the two Honorable Sanctuaries."

The first ᶜAlawī to acquire the name al-Ḥaddād, which literally means "the ironsmith," was Sayyid Aḥmad, son of Abū Bakr. This *sayyid*, who lived in the ninth century of the *Hijra*, took to sitting at the ironsmith's shop in Tarīm much of his time. There happened to be another Sayyid Aḥmad in Tarīm in those days who was well known and had numerous followers. The ironsmith was unable to bear the fact that his friend, Sayyid Aḥmad, whom he knew to be a man of God, was totally ignored by everyone, while his namesake was so renowned. He criticized the *sayyid* so much for this that he answered the Ironsmith one day, "God willing, you shall witness that which will please you." Soon afterwards people began to flock to the shop to greet the *sayyid*, sit with him, and ask for his *du^cā'* (supplications or prayers). It was not long before the ironsmith found himself unable to work in his shop, so crowded it had become. He said, "O Sayyid, this is enough, I am now convinced you are as I thought you were." Thereafter, to differentiate him from the other Sayyid Aḥmad, people took to calling him al-Ḥaddād and so were his descendants named after him.[3]

One of the virtuous *sayyids* of the line of al-Ḥaddād who lived in Tarīm was Sayyid ᶜAlawī ibn Muḥammad al-Ḥaddād. To him on the eve of Ṣafar the fifth of the year 1044 A.H. was born a son whom he named ᶜAbdallāh. At the age of three or four ᶜAbdallāh son of ᶜAlawī suffered from smallpox which left no disfiguring scars, but deprived him of his vision permanently.

Interior of the house where Imām al-Ḥaddād was born

Mausoleum of Ḥabīb ᶜUmar al-ᶜAṭṭās,
one of the Imām's spiritual masters

Chapter 2
THE YOUNG SEEKER

Memorizing the Qur'ān—beginnings on the Sufi path—the Imām's childhood companions—the Imām' masters—the Khirqa or Sufi investiture—influences from the unseen—relationship with Shaykh ᶜAbdal-Qādir al-Jīlānī.

Despite the Imām's frequent castigations of the Hadramī society of his day, the Tarīm environment was still exceedingly favourable to spirituality. The first priority for children was to commit the entire Qur'ān to memory, for which special care was taken to master the rules of correct recitation handed down from generation to generation since the earliest days of Islam. Thus it was that the young ᶜAbdallāh attended the Qur'ān lessons that began every morning soon after the dawn prayer. Once the lesson was over and the sun had risen high above the horizon, he made for a particular mosque where he prayed between one and two hundred *rakᶜas*, a stupendous feat of spiritual ardor for a boy of his age.

In his "Good Manners of the Spiritual Disciple" he writes, "The beginning of the path is a powerful urge that is cast into the heart so as to disturb and unsettle it and drive it to concentrate on God and the Last Abode and turn away from the world." This urge must have been inborn in his case, as is prevalent in the descendants of the Prophet, may God's blessings and peace be on him and his family. This urge must also have been extremely powerful, for already as a child he was a resolute traveler, aware precisely of his destination. Such was his ardor in devotion that his grandmother, Salmā, herself a woman of great saintliness, felt compelled to order him to be gentler on himself. Because his parents echoed her injunctions, filial piety obliged him to comply, albeit reluctantly, and he abandoned many of his devotional activities. Nevertheless, he still prayed his two hundred *rak^{c}as* in the Bā-^{c}Alawī mosque in the company of one of his childhood friends, Sayyid ^{c}Abdallāh Bilfaqīh, after which he fervently petitioned God for the spiritual degree of Imām ^{c}Abdallāh al-^{c}Aydarūs, while his friend asked for the degree of his own grandfather, Sayyid ^{c}Abdallāh ibn Muḥammad, a well known *sayyid* whose grave lies in the Shubayka cemetery in Makka.

His natural disposition presented no obstacle to his spiritual yearning, for, as a certain gnostic[4] *sayyid* who knew him well once said, "He grew up in the *fitra* (the primordial nature), and exhibited perfection in his attributes, both those belonging to the human aspect and those belonging to the elect." The Imām had a constant feeling of his falling short of the ideal of perfection which he strove to achieve. Nevertheless he was aware that his natural disposition was a help and not a hindrance, on the path; his natural appetites and passions were innately such that they never distracted him from the main task. "None of you believes," the Prophet had said, may God's blessings and peace be upon him, "until his passions conform to what I have brought."

The young ^{c}Abdallāh had a few friends who shared his insatiable appetite for knowledge and his profound yearning for the states of gnosis. Three of those deserve special mention since they became great saints in their own right. The first was Sayyid Aḥmad ibn ^{c}Umar al-Hunduwān, the second Sayyid ^{c}Alī ibn ^{c}Abdallāh al-^{c}Aydarūs, and the third, the already mentioned Sayyid ᶜAbdallāh ibn Aḥmad Bilfaqīh. In their company he studied under many scholars and soon mastered the sciences that are the necessary armamentarium of the accomplished scholar. They read the works of Imām al-Ghazālī and other authorities as well as the poetry of Imām al-Sūdī and other Sufis. Some of these works they read as they walked in the streets of Tarīm, going from one place to another, so as not to waste any time. In the company of Sayyid Bilfaqīh, ᶜAbdallāh went out into the surrounding valleys between the sandy hills, where it was peaceful and where they read and memorized the Qur'ān and studied jurisprudence. At night the young ᶜAbdallāh roamed the town, visiting each of its mosques to pray, filling up the basins with water where in the morning people would perform their ablutions, and visiting his ancestors in the cemetery. He and Sayyid al-ᶜAydarūs were joined in a formal bond of brotherhood in the course of one of their visits to the tomb of al-Faqīh al-Muqaddam, whom they were in the habit of visiting together on the eve of each Friday, after which they returned to al-Hujayra mosque to spend the rest of the night reading books. They and Sayyid Aḥmad ibn Hāshim al-Ḥabashī, another of the Imām's childhood friends, were disciples of the great gnostic Imām ᶜUmar ibn ᶜAbdal-Raḥmān alᶜAṭṭās. Sayyid ᶜUmar al-ᶜAṭṭās showed more respect for Imām ᶜAbdallāh al-Ḥaddād, once saying to al-Ḥabashī, "You and Sayyid ᶜAbdallāh have been brought together at the beginning, but will separate at the end." Sayyid al-Ḥabashī later recounted that when they were still studying under Sayyid ᶜUmar, Imām ᶜAbdallāh received his Opening at which time he himself became acutely aware of his own lagging behind. He complained about this concern to their master who first listened attentively, and then proceeded to recite the following passage from the Prophet's *mawlid*, "He and she were united; he and she were connected; her womb enveloped her child; the light of the Chosen One, may God's blessings and peace be upon him, shone forth from her forehead!" At this moment al-Ḥabashī received his Opening. The symbolism used by the master here is quite interesting. The marriage of the Prophet's parents to which this passage refers, is to be understood as the inward connection that occurs between the master's spirit, which is the active pole of the dyad, or father, and the disciple's which is the passive pole, or receptive mother. The child that is conceived by this spiritual marriage is the Opening, that is the "shining forth" of the Prophetic Light and the spiritual rank thus attained.

Sayyid Bilfaqīh was once heard saying, "We grew up together, but he outstripped us.... He was given his Opening in his childhood, when *sūra* Ya-Sīn was recited before him, we could see how greatly it affected him; he wept profusely and was sometimes barely able to [continue] listening to it." His young friends, already with some knowledge of the path, were convinced at the time that he had been given a special Opening related to Ya-Sīn. In effect, this chapter of the Qur'ān remained his constant companion until the end of his life. He recited it many times each day and later had it recited before him in the mosque following each ritual prayer. He also had it recited forty times for the relief of severe hardships and advised everyone to do the same. He was inspired as well with a special supplication to be recited after the *sūra*, which is still in extensive use today.

The Imām's *shaykhs* were numerous, more than a hundred according to a letter he once dictated in answer to a question from one of his disciples. He wrote, "Know that we have met with and taken from numerous people, both Abū ᶜAlawī *sayyids* and others whom we have known in

The Bāᶜ Alawī Mosque in the center of Tarīm

Mausoleum of Shaykh Abū Bakr ibn Salīm at ᶜInat.

Tarīm, other parts of Hadramawt, in the two Noble Sanctuaries, and in the Yemen during our *ḥajj* voyage. Were we to count them they would perhaps exceed one hundred, some of them scholars, others gnostics, others virtuous brothers."

The most important of his masters, from whom he received both formal teaching and spiritual transmission, was the already mentioned al-ᶜAṭṭās, whose master had been Sayyid al-Ḥusayn, son of the great Shaykh Abū-Bakr ibn Sālim. Sayyid al-ᶜAṭṭās invested Imām al-Ḥaddād with the *khirqa*, the cloth that symbolizes spiritual transmission among Sufis. Prior to doing so, however, he made it a condition that he would also receive it from Imām al-Ḥaddād, which the younger *sayyid* was evidently most reluctant to do, as he was in his early twenties when his master was nearing the end of his long life. The elder man insisted, however, and had his way. He also insisted that Imām al-Ḥaddād lead the prayers in his presence and again was reluctantly obeyed. This indicated his recognition of the spiritual stature of Imām al-Ḥaddād and that, in their case, the master-disciple relationship was relative, not total. As Imām al-Ḥaddād was departing from his master's village after one of his visits, a man caught up with him carrying Sayyid ᶜUmar's walking stick, saying that he had been told to hand it over to him. Imām al-Ḥaddād later said that he had received it with gratitude, meaning that he had understood and accepted what was being given to him. He was never heard to state explicitly what exactly it was. However, one may surmise that it meant that he was al-ᶜAṭṭās's spiritual heir and was thus to receive his spiritual power or secret at his death and replace him in his leading role of calling the people to God.

Another great man from whom he received the *khirqa* was Sayyid Muḥammad ibn ᶜAlawī al-Saqqāf who had left Hadramawt for the Hijāz and spent the last years of his life

The Cemetery of Zanbal. The mausoleum on the right hand side of the picture is that of Imām ᶜAbdallah al-ᶜAydarūs, that on the left is that of *Sayyid* Shaykh al-ᶜAydarūs, the open shelter in the middle covers the grave of Imām al-Ḥaddād and his descendants.

in Makka. The two men never met physically, but knew each other through correspondence. When Imām al-Ḥaddād was approximately twenty years old he became preoccupied with three questions for which he could neither find answers in books nor from the men of God whom he knew. Then one day he met with Shaykh Ḥasan Bā-Shuᶜayb coming out from the Bā-ᶜAlawī mosque. He stopped him, for he knew that he was connected to Shaykh Abū Bakr ibn Sālim, and despite the Shaykh's seeming annoyance, put these three questions to him. He received satisfactory answers for two of them and was told to seek the answer for the third with al-Saqqāf. It immediately occurred to him that the Saqqāf in question was no other than the great man in Makka. He wrote to him and effectively received the requested answer. There was further correspondence between the two of them, leading to the Imām's request for the investiture with the *khirqa*. There was a delay in the Makkan *sayyid's* answer, for he felt unable to grant such a request without a direct order from the Prophet, may God's blessings and peace be upon him. He thus travelled to Madina and stood before the Prophet until he became drenched in sweat and a spiritual state came upon him which made him totally unaware of his physical surroundings. Afterwards he came out of the mosque saying that the Prophet had sanctioned the investiture of Sayyid ᶜAbdallāh. He sent him the *khirqa* forthwith by a messenger who reached Tarīm on Friday the fourteenth of Rabīᶜal-Thānī, in the year 1071 A.H., the very day that the master died and was buried in al-Maᶜlā cemetery in Makka, not far from the lady Khadīja. The coincidence of the arrival of the *khirqa* and investiture of Imām al-Ḥaddād with the death of Sayyid Muḥammad has been taken to indicate that he was his spiritual heir.

Another master from whom Imām al-Ḥaddād received the *khirqa* was Sayyid ᶜAqīl ibn ᶜAbdal-Raḥmān al-Saqqāf, whom he calls "the Sufi, the *malāmatī*." "I inwardly intended, when I went to visit him," said Imām al-Ḥaddād, "that I wished to be invested with the *khirqa* of the Sufis from him on that day. When I arrived, he took the cap that was on my head and put it on his, then he put it back on mine saying, 'We have invested you and have never invested anyone else before.'" Clearly this *sayyid* was one of the hidden men of God whose inner state is recognized only by those of equal or nearly equal calibre, indicated by his being said to be a *malāmatī,* a saint of supreme rank whose spiritual state is hidden behind a mundane appearance.

The investiture (*ilbās*) with the *khirqa* (cloth) is the outward expression of the invisible spiritual transmission that takes place between the master and the disciple, or sometimes between two masters. The *khirqa* consists of anything capable of being worn, such as a shawl, mantle, cap, turban, or tunic. The *shaykh* who performs the *ilbās* has the full weight of his spiritual ancestry behind him, consisting of all the links in the chain, which connect him with the Prophet, may God's blessings and peace be upon him.

The ᶜAlawīs recognize three levels to this rite. The first is the *khirqa majāziyya*, and the adjective here means "metaphorical" or "figurative," thereby indicating that this is only outwardly symbolic of the full investiture, while nevertheless allowing those who receive it to enjoy the *baraka* of the *shaykh* in a general way. This is meant for those who are attracted in one way or another to the elect but whose determination, understanding, and effort do not qualify them as actual travelers. "Our investing the common people with the *khirqa* of the Sufis," said the Imām, "is but for *baraka* and imitation. We take the people along the common road, which has today become special." This is why he never refused to invest even the most mundane of people, governors, officials, and merchants. However, for some benefit to be derived from it, he expected some effort on their part. "One should not desire to receive the *khirqa* simply for appearance's sake, and those who seek it as just an outward formality obtain nothing. Rather, it is for the essence of it, which is the bond; and after the investiture one should emulate the one who has bestowed it upon him, even if partly." The same *khirqa* is also granted for *baraka* to those who, although potential travelers, have not yet become truly attached to a master. Says the Imām, "The one whose heart is not yet set on a particular *shaykh* should meet with them all and absorb from their *baraka* until the time he finds his heart collectedly set on one of these masters. Then he should keep his company and surrender his affairs to him." This is the traditional advice given to every potential seeker throughout the ages: "Sit with the masters, drink in their *baraka*, for their mere presence radiates such light that whoever is with them is penetrated by it through and through." Shaykh Muḥammad al-Bajlī is said to have seen the Prophet, may God's blessings and peace be upon him, in a dream vision and asked him which was the best of all deeds? His answer was, "To sit before a saint of God for as long as it takes to milk a goat or cook an egg."[5]

The second level is the *khirqa jawāziyya*, which heralds one's admission to the path and allows the resolute traveler, already attached to the *shaykh* and his spiritual ancestry, to receive from them the kind of support that will allow his efforts to be crowned with success.

The third and highest is the *khirqa ijāziyya*, which confers upon those who receive it the authority to bestow it upon others in the name of the *shaykh*, acting as his deputies and connecting the prospective disciples to the *shaykh* rather than to themselves. This is the kind usually dispensed by the Imām to advanced travelers. It may also be unconditional, in which case it is the *khirqa* of election and indicates that the traveler has reached the goal of the path and become a master in his own right.

The disciples of one *shaykh* may request the *khirqa* from another, not to establish a spiritual bond similar to the original one between them and their own master that cannot be duplicated, but rather to receive the *baraka* of the other *shaykh's* chain, a practice which is perfectly legitimate and even encouraged. On the other hand, requests for repeated investitures by the same *shaykh* are discouraged, since it is the *shaykh*, not the disciple, who knows when and why it should be dispensed. When someone receives it in the presence of others, however, the ᶜAlawī custom is to extend the investiture to all those present.

As Imām al-Ḥaddād grew up he became very fond of the poetry of ᶜUmar ibn al-Fāriḍ, the Egyptian Sufi known as the Sultan of Lovers. He also studied the works of his ᶜAlawī ancestors and those of the Shādhilīs, such as ibn ᶜAṭā'illāh's *Laṭā'if al-Minan*[6] and his *Ḥikam*[7]. Much later, he was heard saying, "Had I continued to read the books of the Shādhilīs, great things would have happened, but I was commanded by someone from the Intermediary World to leave them and read the books of Ghazālī." Mention of the Intermediary World refers us to the powerful spiritual bond between the Imām and his ancestors, for he had an immense love for them, lived in the conviction that every good came from following in their footsteps, knew their biographies in detail, and frequently praised them in his poems. He was an assiduous visitor to the cemetery where most of them are buried. Some of his visits were witnessed by his contemporaries and later recounted to his chief biographer and are thus preserved on record. One such story was told by a man who lived near al-Hujayra mosque where the Imām had his retreat. Every night he saw him leave the mosque and head toward that of Shaykh al-Meḥḍār. One night he followed him at a distance and saw him walk alone, with neither guide nor staff, yet never straying off the road, nor even hesitating. They eventually reached Zanbal and the man waited outside for the Imām to return. It took him a long time to reappear and then he took a different route back, stopping at three or four mosques on the way to pray a few *rakᶜas* in each. Then, to his surprise, he saw the Imām turn to him, call him by his name, and say, "Will you not stop being inquisitive? Now go back!"

Another recounted how he was once sitting on his own at night in the mosque after everyone had gone home when he saw the Imām come in and although he had not made a sound, call him and after having talked with him for a while, say, "I want to visit the cemetery tonight." "Yes, Sayyidī," he replied. They went out together and as they neared the cemetery, the Imām said, "Remain firm and do not be frightened by whatever you might see or hear." "As long as I am with you," the man said, "I shall remain firm." When they reached the tomb of al-Faqīh al-Muqaddam, the Imām said, *"As-salāmu ᶜAlaykum."* "And by God," said the man, "I heard his greeting being answered from all the tombs!" He was greatly terrified. Placing his hand on his chest, the Imām said, "Fear not, these are the living, do you think that they are dead? We are the dead, they are the living." Some of the man's terror abated at that, but the Imām nevertheless kept his palm on his chest until they rose to depart. It is perhaps this verse of the Qur'ān that the Imām had in mind. *"Think not that those who were slain for the sake of God are dead, they are alive with their Lord and He provides for them."* [3:169] It is well known that even the ordinary dead are aware of what happens in our world and of those who visit them. The Prophet, may God's blessings and peace be upon him, said, "None passes by the grave of his brother, whom he knew in the world, and greets him but that he recognizes him and greets him back."[8] Only in exceptional circumstances can one hear the voices of the dead. One of the Companions of the Prophet, may God's blessings and peace be upon him, once pitched his tent at night in a certain spot, unaware that this was a grave. He heard a voice reciting *sūra* Tabārak, so he rushed back to the Prophet, may God's blessings and peace be upon him, only to be told that this was the voice of another Companion who had passed away and that *sūra* Tabārak protects those who read it in profusion in this world from the torment of the grave.[9] It was the *baraka* of the presence of Imām al-Ḥaddād that permitted his companion to hear what he would not have heard otherwise.

Yet another man recounted how he once visited the cemetery on the eve of ᶜArafāt and found the Imām sitting there on his own, before the tomb of al-Faqīh al-Muqaddam. He joined him and was taken by him on a tour of the cemetery, visiting al-Faqīh and those around him, followed by al-Saqqāf, al Meḥdār, al-ᶜAydarūs, and those in their vicinity. Then the Imām asked his companion to depart, entered the mausoleum of al-ᶜAydarūs, and shut the door behind him.

One reason for the Imām's frequent visits to the cemetery was that although he had received guidance and spiritual transmission from many a great master, his *shaykh* of the Opening seems to have been none other than Imām ᶜAbdallāh al-ᶜAydarūs, who had lived in Tarīm and died in 865 A.H. Although rather rare, it is not unknown for great men of God to have had for a master a *shaykh* already departed from this world, since such spiritual transmission is possible when certain conditions are fulfilled. Furthermore, to become great saints they must all reach the stage where they receive this transmission directly from the Prophet, may God's blessings and peace be upon him.

It is told that the relationship between Imām al-Ḥaddād and Imām al-ᶜAydarūs began when his mother took him, shortly after his birth, to the tomb of Imām al-ᶜAydarūs. The Imām came out as she watched, took the child in his hands, and sucked his tongue. This was the Imām's first spiritual transmission. The second was at the age of seven, again from al-ᶜAydarūs, whom he again saw sitting outside his tomb, but this time inside the mausoleum. He extended his hand to him and gave him the oath of allegiance. Both these occurrences pertain to *ᶜālam al-mithāl*, the world of subtle images, and are not as rare as one might think, even in the lives of much lesser saints. This relationship between al-Ḥaddād and al-ᶜAydarūs was later confirmed in a dream that the Imām thus recounted: "I saw in a dream vision that I came to the mosque of the House of Abī ᶜAlawī. Shaykh ᶜAbdallāh al-ᶜAydarūs and his brother ᶜAlī were sitting between the two pillars on the left of the *miḥrāb*. I walked up to them and each of them wanted the other to receive my allegiance; then al-ᶜAydarūs came to me and put something into my mouth which made me lose my senses. Thereafter, I never set my sight on something without obtaining it." And another man of God said that he saw in a dream vision, two fountains springing from the tomb of Sayyid ᶜAbdallāh al-ᶜAydarūs. He asked, "Who are those two fountains for?" and was told, "They are for Sayyid ᶜAbdallāh al Ḥaddād."

There were many other spiritual influences from the Intermediary World, some of which are more important than others. The Imām was heard saying, "We are indebted in this matter to four people from the Intermediary World: al-Faqīh al-Muqaddam, Shaykh ᶜAbdal-Raḥmān al-Saqqāf, Shaykh ᶜUmar al-Meḥdār, and Shaykh ᶜAbdallāh ibn Abū Bakr al-ᶜAydarūs. As for now, we take from the Prophet, may God's blessings and peace be upon him, without intermediary."

The first mentioned, al-Faqīh al-Muqaddam, was and still remains the master of all subsequent ᶜAlawīs. A man of formidable spiritual stature, he was said by Sayyid ᶜAbdal-Raḥmān al-Saqqāf to have been the Pole of his time. He received the heritage of knowledge and spirituality of his ᶜAlawī ancestors and added to it the investiture with the *khirqa* of Sufism from the illustrious Shaykh Abū Madian through the intermediary of two emissaries, both gnostic *shaykhs*, dispatched by Abū Madian from North Africa for the purpose. Abū Madian's *khirqa* comes from a chain that includes al-Ghazālī and al-Junayd, as well as Shaykh ᶜAbdal-Qādir al-Jīlānī, whom Abu Madian is said to have met on ᶜArafāt during *ḥajj*.

Imām al-Ḥaddād's relationship with al-Faqīh al-Muqaddam was extremely intimate, and he was once heard saying, "I never do anything until I receive a sign from the Real, Exalted be He, or the Prophet, may God's blessings and peace be upon him, or Sayyidunā al-Faqīh al-Muqaddam Muḥammad ibn ᶜAlī Bā-ᶜAlawī." Very frequently he was also heard saying, "If the Prophet permits us, we shall do such a thing." It was said by many of his companions that Imām al-Ḥaddād in his young days frequently came under the sway of spiritual states during sessions of remembrance. He sometimes became lost in ecstasy and the only way to return him to ordinary consciousness was to carry him to the tomb of al-Faqīh and lay him there for a while. He was also frequently seen sitting before the grave for so long that his clothes became thoroughly soaked with sweat, though he was so engrossed that he seemed not to feel it at all.

As for Imām ᶜAbdal-Raḥmān al-Saqqāf, he was called the Second Muqadddam (*al-Muqaddam al-Thānī*), as he was another major nexus in the ᶜAlawī chain. His sons were all great men, Shaykh ᶜUmar al-Meḥdār being one of them, and al-ᶜAydarūs's father, Sayyid Abū Bakr al-Sakrān another.

Another gnostic *sayyid* who looked after him from the Intermediary world was Aḥmad ibn Muḥammad al-Ḥabashī, who died in 1038 H., six years before Imām ᶜAbdallāh's birth, and was a disciple of Shaykh Abū Bakr ibn Sālim. He was Imām al-Ḥaddād's maternal great-grandfather. When Sayyid ᶜAlawī al-Ḥaddād, Imām al-Ḥaddād's father, visited him before his marriage, he was told, "Your children are our children, they are blessed." These words were understood by Sayyid ᶜAlawī many years later when the young ᶜAbdallāh began to show signs of early sanctity. Imām al-Ḥaddād said, "I saw in a dream vision the gnostic *sayyid*, Aḥmad ibn Muḥammad al-Ḥabashī. He invested me with the *khirqa* of the Sufis, the Bā-ᶜAbbād well known hat, then on top of it the Bā-ᶜAlawī illustrious hat, then he asked me who were the living? I answered that the living were those who are alive with the gnosis of God the Exalted, and he said, 'You have spoken the truth!'"

Another great man of whom the Imām spoke of as very closely connected with him was Shaykh ᶜAbdal-Qādir when he said, "My affair was founded and erected on the great ones, among whom are Shaykh ᶜAbdal-Qādir al-Jīlānī, al-Faqīh al-Muqaddam, Shaykh ᶜAbdal-Raḥmān al-Saqqāf, and Shaykh ᶜAbdallāh ibn Abū Bakr al-ᶜAydarūs." This time he quoted them in chronological order and implied that there were more unmentioned *shaykhs*.

The illustrious Shaykh ᶜAbdal-Qādir, one of the greatest Sufi masters of all time, is at the origin of innumerable Sufi chains. He flourished in Baghdad in the sixth century of the *Hijra*, six centuries before Imām al-Ḥaddād. Yet the Imām was to say, "We have taken from Shaykh ᶜAbdal-Qādir both through intermediaries and without. We are also connected to him by way of the ties of kinship between the People of the House as well as otherwise." The intermediaries in question are the men of God constituting the chain of transmission connecting the two men, both via Shaykh Abū Madian as well as other masters. There seems to have been more than a passing affinity between the spiritual states of Imām al-Ḥaddād and Shaykh ᶜAbdal-Qādir. The Imām was once overheard, in his beginnings, relating to another *sayyid* a dream where he had seen "Shaykh ᶜAbdal-Qādir bringing him a letter from his Lord, which was difficult to open." The implication of this is that despite the fact that the *shaykh* was one of his mentors and was carrying a letter from the Divine Presence to him, he was nonetheless unaware of its contents which were a secret between the Imām and his Lord. "He asked for my permission to read it to me," continued the Imām, "and I was delighted. He read to me my states, then said, 'My Lord bid me do this O Sayyid ᶜAbdallāh, so strive with utmost ardor, for you shall soon obtain 'my spiritual degree.' I hope that God shall make a reality of the words of Shaykh ᶜAbdal-Qādir, and this is our utmost wish." To confirm this, one of the Imām's companions saw in a dream vision that a man he knew who had passed away was saying to him, "The station of Sayyidī ᶜAbdallāh al-Ḥaddād is like that of Sayyidī ᶜAbdal-Qādir al-Jīlānī." To which Sayyid Aḥmad ibn Zayn al-Ḥabashī was later to add the following remark: "The state of Sayyidī ʿAbdallāh was that of Shaykh ʿAbdal-Qādir in his youth, as for now, nobody knows." The Imām also indicated that he had inherited the inward function and attributes of Shaykh ʿAbdal-Qādir saying, "Shaykh ʿAbdal-Qādir al-Jīlānī sat on a carpet that was folded up after him and never unfolded again until the time of Shaykh ʿAbdallāh ibn Abū Bakr al-ʿAydarūs. It was then folded up until our time when it was unfolded for us. It shall again be folded when we disappear from this world and none shall sit on it again, unless there remains someone before whom people still feel shame." The last sentence refers to those men of God before whom those still capable of feeling shame are fearful of being exposed. Some of them might yet be worthy of being the Imām's spiritual heirs.

In 1117 A.H., when the Yāfeʿī tribesmen invaded Hadramawt and tyrannized its people, Imām al-Ḥaddād composed a poem in which he complained to Shaykh ʿAbdal-Qādir about his long absence, giving clear indications that he was used to meeting him face to face and asking him to intercede on behalf of the people for the relief of their hardships. In the same year he also composed a poem in praise of the Prophet, may God's blessings and peace be upon him, again asking him to help the people in their trials. This poem is still recited at times of hardship by the people of Hadramawt and elsewhere, so powerful a prayer it is.

There were two inevitable questions to arise in the minds of the disciples of the Imām under these circumstances. First, why should he call on Shaykh ʿAbdal-Qādir when Tarīm was full of great ʿAlawīs, and secondly, who was the greater man, Shaykh ʿAbdal-Qādir or al-Faqīh al-Muqaddam? The answer the Imām gave to the first question was that his ᶜAlawī ancestors were perfectly aware of what had befallen the land, since it was happening in their vicinity. There was therefore no need to call upon them, because they were certain to have already interceded with God on behalf of the people to alleviate their hardships. His answer to the second question as dictated in a letter and subsequently quoted in "The Sublime Treasures" was as follows: "Both al-Faqīh al-Muqaddam and Shaykh ᶜAbdal-Qādir were great Īmāms; they were all-encompassing Poles and *Sunnī sharīfs*. Both are among the Foremost and the Drawn Near. We benefit and depend more on al-Faqīh, since he is the father and the *shaykh* around whom everything in this region revolves, both as concerns us and as concerns others. They are equal in station, however, Shaykh ᶜAbdal-Qādir is better known in this world and al-Faqīh in the Intermediary World."

The result of such concentrated spiritual solicitude was that, since his childhood, Imām al-Ḥaddād was respected by his elders and treated differently from the other boys of his age. He often visited an elderly *sayyid* by the name of ᶜAbdal-Raḥmān ᶜAydīd, who used to say, "Look at me, for I have seen Sayyid Abū Bakr ibn Sālim, and those who have seen him shall enter the Garden." Both the old man and his son were saints and gnostics of the first order. When al-Ḥaddād came to visit them, they sat the child near them on the couch, a privilege no other child was granted, and they usually greeted him by saying, "Welcome to the Master of the Group." As he grew up into his early twenties he was recognized by the saints of his time as of already considerable spiritual rank. A disciple of the *majdhūb*, or ecstatic, Sayyid Muḥammad ibn Abū Bakr al-ᶜAydarūs related how he once consulted his *shaykh* about a certain matter at which he was told to go and consult Sayyid ᶜAbdallāh al-Ḥaddād, then to comply with whatever he advised. He headed for the retreat of al-Hujayra mosque looking for the Imām, whom he had never seen before. As soon as he entered the mosque, Imām al-Ḥaddād called him using both his first and family names. "Come here!" he said. He permitted him to talk, listened to him and then gave him the requested advice.

Chapter 3
STATIONS AND STATES

The dense veils, ailments of the heart—the nine stations of certainty: repentance, fear and hope, patience and gratitude, detachment and reliance, love and contentment.

In the Imām's *Dīwān* are found the following verses in which he mentions the veils standing between the ordinary human being and his Lord. Dense veils are followed by subtle veils, the piercing of which leads out of the created universe and into the Ocean of Divine Lights.

The secret of God is hidden pervading the universe and man;
Cross therefore the dense veils leaving them behind, diligently
And cross the subtle veils going through them, undeceived.
Once you ascend beyond the Lote Tree of secrets and Destiny
Halt and await a sign from the knowledge of the Command[10], take heed!

The dense veils here signify the various ailments afflicting the heart, those upon which Imām al-Ghazālī expounds at length in that part of the *Iḥyā'* dealing with "Ruinous Things" and which Imām al-Ḥaddād wrote about more concisely in "*al-Naṣā'iḥ.*" He is reported to have said, "When a man sinks lower than his human rank by being dominated by passions and appetites to the extent of losing all nobility, he becomes the animal corresponding to that which dominates him. For each animal is dominated and characterized by one of these qualities. Whenever one of the Children of Adam is dominated by one of these, he becomes identified with the animal whose attribute it is. Should he then wish to reach God, he must strive to reach the human level which consists of that which is the human prerogative, then further strive to reach Him." These lower appetites are the first obstacles that hinder a seeker setting out on the path. Most of these relate to the physical level, but some pertain to the next level, namely that of the psyche. These are usually lumped together under the term passion (*hawā*). "Passion," said the Imām, "blinds one to the truth. Just as a hard blowing wind blinds the eyesight, so does passion blind insight to the truth. Passion is the powerful inclination of the soul toward something illusory."

Passions divert a man from his concentration on the Real and detract from his sincerity. They are the hidden kind of idolatry that the Qur'ān warns about, *"Have you seen he who has taken his passion for his God?"* [25:43] The most insidious and thus dangerous form of idolatry is what the Sufis designate by the term *riyā'*, which we shall render as ostentation. Sincerity and ostentation are at the opposite poles of a scale ranging from total sincerity, that of the *ṣiddīqūn*, to total insincerity, that of the hypocrites or *munāfiqūn*. "Ostentation and sincerity differ from one person to another," said the Imām, "the sincerity of the common people not being that of the elect, which, in turn, is not that of the 'elect of the elect.' The sincerity of some may amount to ostentation for others." And he also said, "Sincerity is difficult, you may secretly believe, between yourself and God, that your state is blameworthy, but when someone calls you by that very name you become angry." The subtle nature of this ailment requires extreme vigilance if one is to avoid its perils. This is why the Imām was ever intent on bringing the people around him into awareness of it. On one occasion, when a man came seeking his permission to build a mosque, a praiseworthy endeavor, the Imām counseled him, "If your intention in building it is purely for the sake of God, then we shall not prevent you from building it, but if it is not, then do not build it!" "My intention is sincere," the man replied. The Imām continued, "Consider then, if you were to build it, expend much effort and spend much money, and then, when it is completed, it is not attributed to you but to someone else, so that it is said 'This is that man's mosque' and it becomes known as such, and you are never mentioned in connection with it, would you find your ego submitting to this?" The man reflected briefly, then said, "I do not see my ego submitting to this." The Imām then commanded, "Leave it then, for your intention is not sincere!" On another occasion, when one of his disciples, who happened to be fasting on that day, asked his permission to visit a *sayyid* who had fallen ill, he reprimanded him, "How can you go when you are fasting? Do you wish to inform them that you are fasting?"

The Imām's instructions to his disciples on avoidance of this particular pitfall are set out as follows: "Know that to display [one's devotions] is better for those who are at no risk of ostentation hoping that some of their brother believers will emulate them. But concealing one's devotions is better for those who do fear ostentation. Concealment is also better for those who are safe from ostentation, because their hearts are pure, but expect none to follow them, because their true state is hidden, and *vice versa*."

Even the virtuous are not altogether safe. "The saint is hidden from the common people," said the Imām, "but known to his peers and to himself. The saint only wishes for obscurity; should he ever come to take pleasure in fame he is dispossessed." And, "Saints do not like the people to come to them, the one who does is one who still harbors traces of ostentation. Even the one who wishes for a crowd at his funeral is an ostentatious seeker of posthumous fame." Imām al-Ḥaddād advised them, "Cast yourselves down to the ground. If your state with God is satisfactory, this will elevate you even more."

He bid those who came to him, however, not to accuse themselves of ostentation whenever incidental evil thoughts pass through their minds. "For in the hearts of weak men numerous are the thoughts of this nature until the heart becomes free of [all attachment to] creation; and scarce they are in the hearts of the virtuous, but when they do occur such people immediately turn away from them."

As for the subtle veils, these are the stations of certainty that one has to acquire to deserve to be called a "man" (*rajul*) and experience the resulting spiritual states. Sufis often speak of these, for as the Imām said, "A man is not a man until he comes to possess something of every part of humanity, and every part of his ego loses something, each according to his degree and rank with God the Exalted. Saints differ in this respect, the supreme one being the Pole, for he is more perfect in this than anyone else. None has ever received a greater share of this than the Prophet, may God's blessings and peace be upon him. The more perfect the servant becomes, that is, the more dominated he is by the spiritual side, the more his ego will lose its passions, even to the extent that they may appear to have been lost altogether."

These stations, which are the same virtues mentioned by Imām al-Ghazālī in that part of the *Iḥyā'* dealing with "Saving Things," were mentioned by Imām al-Ḥaddād in another of his poems. "The stations of certainty," says the poem, "are nine to know and master." It then mentions repentance, followed by the four pairs: "fear and hope," "fortitude and gratitude," "renunciation and reliance," and finally "love and contentment." These nine stations are explained by Imām al-Ḥaddād in the last six chapters of *The Book of Assistance*, preceded by a chapter on scrupulousness (*wara*ᶜ) which remains one of the best works ever written on the subject.

Scrupulousness is defined as the avoidance of not only everything that is legally forbidden but also everything that is suspect. When practiced with sincerity it extends to every aspect of life, and this is why the Imām exemplified this quality to perfection in both his worldly and religious affairs. He endeavored to be well informed about everything that either came into his possession or proceeded from it. This, however, he did without exaggeration and without obsessively prying into the affairs of others. He kept to the golden mean, which in this context consists in being circumspect, neither over-inquisitive nor neglectful. For instance, whenever he employed someone for a particular task he always paid them double the wage agreed upon. That is, he paid them according to their hearts' desire rather than the work done, for he wished to avoid arousing any ill feelings, whether justified or not. He also watched his every word, spoke only when strictly necessary, and then only with either a remembrance of God, profitable knowledge, good advice, or to put his guests at ease. He frequently refrained from giving legal opinions, instead passing the inquiry on to other scholars. Whenever he quoted another scholar's words, he always attributed them to their author, and he always observed the limits of what he considered safe to be said publicly. His state was in complete conformity with Imām al-Ghazālī's statement that, "the scrupulousness of the *ṣiddīqūn* is to take from God and for His sake, and abstain from whatever is not from God, and not for His sake." As some of the great gnostics who surrounded Imām al-Ḥaddād have pointed out, he never saw other than God as the giver whenever given something, and since he was totally detached and indifferent to the world, he accepted strictly for His sake. Means and intermediaries were for him transparent, and his perception of the One Power acting within them was constant.

According to Sufi consensus, the first station without which there can be no journey is repentance, which means to turn away from whatever is wrong in one's behavior and resolve never again to repeat such acts. This is the common people's repentance. For the seeker, repentance is to abandon habitual comforts and neglectfulness and resolve to adhere to the *Sunna* as much as possible both in acts of worship and, more difficult still, in behavior towards others. As for the traveler, he must learn to restrain his ego and prevent it from angry and vindictive responses, even when wronged. At a later stage, repentance becomes the remorse and frustration felt with each breath that is not accompanied with the remembrance of God, with each instant of distraction, then perceived as unforgivable ingratitude. "The common people repent from sins," said Dhuʾl-Nūn, "but the elect repent from distraction." As for the elect of the elect, repentance is nothing short of the total severance of all attachment to created beings and exclusive concentration on the Real. The Imām expresses this attitude thus, "For the men of God who divest themselves of all attachment to the worlds, sin is to attend to other than God, whatever this other may be. We see them fearfully fleeing to God and seeking refuge in Him from states which, if experienced by others, would be considered great devotions."

For even within an act of worship there lurks the danger of attending to other than God. The Imām continues, "They may notice that they have come to find comfort in their virtuous acts and to rely on them, and they then turn back to God, repentant, asking for forgiveness."

The next two stations, hope and fear, are the driving forces motivating energies, which propel the traveler forward. "The basis of hope," wrote the Imām, "is the heart's knowledge of the immensity of God's mercy and generosity, the magnitude of His favors and kindness, and His gracious promise to those who obey Him. This knowledge generates a state of joyous relief which is termed hope." He is also reported to have said, "We have such hope in God and think so well of Him that, were as much as the eye of a needle of this to appear to the people, they would abandon works and depend on it." Sometimes the Imām uses the word 'hope' in a more profound way, to include the state of intimacy that follows upon the mastery of that station and is the result of the unveiling of the Divine Attributes of Beauty.

As for fear, the Imām's focus on it is evident in his books, but he once put it into perspective by saying, "Our most dominant state is hope in God and thinking well of Him, Exalted be He, both as concerns us and all other Muslims. However, God has given us the tongue of fear out of compassion for the common people, for they are prone to be greatly deluded about the King, the Compeller. Our most dominant state is hope, even as concerns the transgressors of various sects." The sects he refers to are none other than the various unorthodox groups such as the different kinds of *Shīʿa* and the *Khawārij*. "The basis of fear," he writes, "is the heart's knowledge of the Majesty of God, His invincible might, His independence of any of His creatures, and the severe punishments and painful torments with which He has threatened those who disobey Him and disobey His commands. This awareness generates a state of apprehension which is termed fear." The fear of the elect, however, is not so much their fear of hell as that of the awesome Divine Presence, awe being the state consequent upon the mastery of the station of fear. And this is how the Imām was seen weeping whenever a fear inspiring passage was recited before Him, whether from the Qur'ān, *Ḥadith*, or Sufi poetry. Gnostics know very well that they are the elect of God, but they know equally well that there is no restricting the Divine will and power and that they can never be completely certain that they are not about to be dispossessed of all their spiritual gifts.

As for fortitude and gratitude, the Imām once commented to one of his disciples, "When you are afflicted with something that you are able to endure patiently, then do not abandon fortitude, which is the station of the Companions of the Right Hand. Anxiety is characteristic of the rebellious believers, and gratitude, which is higher, corresponds to the station of the Drawn Near." He also stated, "Gratitude during hardship is to have fortitude and to refrain from objecting, while gratitude during affluence is to give away and to demonstrate respect for the [Divine] favors."

These two stations of fortitude and gratitude are often regarded as the two basic components of faith. From this perspective, all other stations would be included in these two. There is a famous story that illustrates quite pleasantly how love and contentment, for instance, merge with fortitude. Once when Shaykh al-Shiblī was thought to be crazed and was incarcerated in a hospital, his friends came to visit him. He inquired, "Who are you?" and they replied "Those who love you and have come to visit you," whereupon he proceeded to pelt them with stones. Upon seeing them flee in dismay, he shouted at them, "You liars! Had you really been those who love me, you would have patiently endured my test!"

Fortitude is said by Imām al-Ḥaddād to be of four kinds, namely patient perseverance in acts of obedience and renouncing sins, and patient endurance of unpleasant happenings and detachment from worldly desires. As far as he was personally concerned, he had no great need for much endurance to persevere in acts of remembrance, for remembrance was the very stuff of which his consciousness was made. Nor did he find great difficulty in resisting temptations, whether sinful or merely superfluous, for indifference to these was second nature to him. As for unpleasant experiences, he was never heard to complain when adversity struck. When both his parents died, five days apart, followed by his closest spiritual master in the course of the same year, he wrote an impressive letter to his brother in India, informing him of what had happened and recommending fortitude. He began by reminding him of the Qurᶜānic passages enjoining fortitude and detailing its merits. He then pointed out that such events are but an indication of the real worth of his world, further reminding him that nothing takes place save by Divine decree and that only those who trust in God's wisdom and compassion, resigning themselves contentedly to His will find peace of heart. Only then did he inform his brother that their father had died after a short illness, followed five days later by their mother. Then he bid him thank God that they died uttering the *Shahāda, Lā ilāha illa'llāh*, and had been satisfied with their son and were praying for him.

The Imām suffered much at the hands of some of Tarīm's governors, as well as other people who resented him. He seldom complained about them and discouraged his disciples from complaining, since within such hardships are hidden divine gifts such as purification from sins, illumination of the heart, refining of character and maturation of the virtues, and, for the already refined, spiritual openings and a constant rise in degree. He also exhibited great patience in sitting with his visitors, humoring them, and attending to their needs. Towards the end of his life, he was afflicted with the loss of his hearing, about which he was never heard to complain. He once told Sayyid Aḥmad ibn Zayn al-Ḥabashī that "fever has been in my body for fifteen years, never leaving me, yet not even the people of my household know of it."

As for gratitude, the Imām wrote, "The basis for thankfulness is that the heart be aware that such [Divine] favors are from God alone, and nothing comes to one through one's own ability and power but solely through God's grace and mercy. The definition of thankfulness is to use each one of His favors in His obedience." This then is the basis of gratitude, to recognize that each breath, each movement, each thought, and each pleasure has no source other than the Divine will and power. This leaves the servant with no achievement that he is able to claim for his own and forces him to remain ever watchful lest he expend some of these favors in that which displeases his Lord. It is said that al-Junayd was once playing as a child in the presence of his uncle, Shaykh Sarī al-Saqatī, while the latter and his guests were conversing about gratitude. He asked the boy, "Child, what is gratitude?" and his answer was, "Not to use God's favors in disobeying Him." Al-Junayd was one of those who, like Imām al-Ḥaddād, was born a saint and had therefore received mastery in this station from childhood. The Imām was ever full of praises for his Lord, ever reminding others to be thankful and to reflect on the innumerable Divine favors without which life itself would be impossible. The great spiritual openings that he received as a young man only led him to intensify his worship and ascetic efforts. In this, as in all other matters, he was a true follower of his ancestor the Prophet, may God's blessings and peace be upon him, who stood all night in prayer until his feet swelled up, answering ᶜĀ'isha's question as to why he did this with, "Should I not be a thankful servant?"

As for the two stations of renunciation and reliance, Imām al-Ghazālī states that "knowledge brings to fruition a state, and the state brings to fruition a station." The explanation of this was given by Imām al-Ḥaddād in *Gifts for the Seeker*, using the station of renunciation as an example. He writes, "Know that renunciation is one of the noble stations. It is established on the basis of the knowledge of what is stated in the Book, the *Sunna*, and what the virtuous men of this nation say, by way of disparagement of the world, criticism of those who chase after it, and praise for those who turn away from it and are more intent on the Hereafter. Following this, if one is given to succeed, one's heart is affected in such a way as to compel one to renounce the world and instead desire only the Hereafter. Knowledge thus comes first, while its consequence is the *state*. Then there appear from the bodily organs and limbs acts that indicate the presence of this effect, such as abandoning the pursuit of worldly riches and accumulation of material things, persevering in those good works which bring advantage in the next life, and so on. This way of life then comes in contact with contrary influences, including the insinuations of the devil and the ego, which encourage desire for the world. Following this onslaught, one's good state may then change, waver, or weaken, it may at times vanish completely, which is why it is termed a *state*. But when it becomes firmly established, is reinforced, and its roots become so deeply implanted in the heart that no passional thoughts are capable of affecting or shaking it, it is termed a *station*."

Attaining to a station thus implies a certain degree of mastery, and the *Sublime Treasures* defines mastery as "complete stability and firm establishment in a station such that the possessor of it never wavers, never changes, and is never overwhelmed." Since "a servant may possess mastery over some but not all stations, he may for instance have mastered the stations of sincerity and renunciation, but not those of reliance and love." Only the one who is granted mastery of all nine stations may be considered a perfect saint. This was the Imām's condition and his mastery of the station of renunciation had been detectable almost since childhood. He then wore nothing but the coarsest clothes and ate nothing but the most frugal food, yet he did not seem to have expended a great deal of effort struggling against his ego in those respects. "I have had no appetite for food for a very long time," he was later to say, "I eat only to conform," meaning thereby that he wished to appear to do what other people did and humor his family. He was also heard to say, "We should now be counted with the dead, for all our worldly appetites have died and we find in us not the slightest inclination nor desire for anything of this world, whether it be food, clothes, or any other thing; and in all these I find no pleasure. However, when food is placed before us we eat what we can to conform. This has been our state for some time now. Prior to this, I had for these things a very weak inclination which has now disappeared, even though you may observe me behaving and speaking differently with the people. The Prophet, may God's blessings and peace be upon him, has said, 'Die before you die!'" He once remarked that those who come to know the illusory nature of the world become detached from it even though they may be disbelievers who expect no Day of Judgment. He said, "All religions have united in vilifying it, yet all the communities to whom those religions were sent are united in loving it." And he remarked that as much as a third of the Qur'ān is aimed at dispraising the world and encouraging people to renounce it.

Renunciation was said by Imām Aḥmad ibn Ḥanbal to be of three degrees. The first is to renounce what is sinful or unlawful, the renunciation of the common people. The second is to renounce what is licit but superfluous, the renunciation of the elect. The third is to renounce everything that may divert the servant from God, and this belongs to the gnostics. "Renunciation is the forerunner of felicity, the manifestation of providence, and the sign of sanctity," wrote Imām al-Ḥaddād in *The Book of Assistance*. This does not mean total outward divestment from worldly goods and means, but total inward detachment from them, so that, "one does not rejoice for what one has, nor mourn for what one has not." He was once heard saying that the jubilation experienced on obtaining a worldly thing is a sign that both one's reason and one's upholding of religion were flawed and wanting, for an increase or a decrease in either one means a corresponding response in the Hereafter. He also stated that true detachment means that one should be indifferent whether one is receiving or giving, and higher than that, that one should be more pleased with giving than with receiving.

The Imām was not only entirely detached from material things, but he was also extremely averse to publicity and its consequences. "I detest eminence and fame by nature," he said, "the most desirable state for me, that which is my wish and aim, is to roam the desert and the lifeless wildernesses, but I was prevented from this so that the people might benefit from me." His concern to avoid publicity led him in his youth to remain secluded in retreat at al-Hujayra mosque. On Fridays he would depart from the Grand Mosque[11] immediately after the prayer was over and lock himself in the place of retreat. Often when people knocked he did not open. At a later stage he declared, "We find no pleasure in conversing with people." Yet it fell to him to sit with them and instruct them, and he was enjoined to do so in his early twenties. He complied, for he could not do otherwise, but it remained a great burden, and in 1110 A.H. he wrote: "By God! I now see myself as a caged bird who has extricated himself until only his heel remains caught in the cage. Since this is now my condition I no longer harbor any remaining desire to sojourn in the world; and I grant no permission to any of my companions to offer me anything

Al-Hujayra Mosque where the Imām lived
and had his retreat in his younger days.

of the world or make mention of any of its affairs." At a later period in his life he is reported to have said, 'My nature has always been averse to conversing about worldly matters, and this has now become accentuated thanks to age and debility. It is also averse to publicity and the formalities imposed by having to deal with people. Let none consult me about worldly matters, nor even make mention of them in my presence, for it would be inappropriate; speak only of the life to come. As for this world, you should consult other than us. It should suffice you that we have come out and stooped for your sake...." Despite this, they persisted in frequently consulting him about all kinds of worldly matters and he did advise and help. The distance that he felt between his own state and everyone else's was enormous and he always made allowances for that. "I have no preoccupation with this world, but I can well believe that others do. There is so much grief in my heart that were it to be divided among the population of Tarīm they would all flee. There is not one hair in me that sways for or desires other than God, Exalted be He!" The grief here mentioned is part of that burning Divine love that the gnostics experience, fuelled by longing and yearning, true to the extent that the heart is free from all that is not the Beloved.

Speaking about reliance, the Imām said, "I have abandoned myself and taken refuge in my Lord, and I am thus unconcerned about provision and have no thought for it." In the knowledge that the Divine treasury is ever full, that Divine solicitude is guaranteed to every creature in the universe, and that to rely on other than God is the very definition of infidelity, the Imām had committed himself entirely to his Lord's mercy. "Know that the basis of reliance on God," he writes, "is the heart's knowledge that all matters are in God's Hand, whether beneficial or harmful, unpleasant or pleasant, and were all creatures to unite to benefit someone, they would benefit him only in the way that God has already decreed for him…." He also adds, "The one whose reliance is sincere has three marks. The first is that he neither hopes in nor fears other than God. The sign of this is that he upholds the truth in the presence of those who usually arouse hope or fear in the people, such as governors and rulers. The second is that worrying about his sustenance never enters his heart because of his confidence in God's guarantee, so that his heart is as tranquil when in need as when his need has been fulfilled, or even more. The third is that his heart does not become disturbed in fearful situations." On one occasion he stated that his way was "To put our needs to God, then accept whatever He sends us at the hands of those of His servants whom He pleases." At another time he mentioned, "When we keep and save for others, that is for our family and the needy, our way is ᶜUmariyya, which means to measure and put order into each matter and place each thing in its rightful place, even though we ourselves care nothing for them. ᶜUmar used to keep order and proportion on behalf of Abū-Bakr, since Abū Bakr was such that whenever he was asked for something by someone with any right to it at all he granted it, whereas ᶜUmar took priorities into account and was very skilful in such assessments, desiring nothing for himself. Had we had neither wives nor children we would have saved nothing, nor ever gone to sleep with anything still remaining in the house."

One of his disciples recounted how the Imām served his guests with his usual ample generosity in a year when there had been a drought and prices had soared. Just as the disciple was wondering about it, he was addressed thus by the Imām, "Be not surprised, there are other matters of mine which may surprise you even more. I have little to do with this, I am but commanded to act thus, and in this my example is not to be followed unless it be by someone who has been granted as much [reliance] as I have." That is, someone who has achieved similar mastery of the station of reliance.

Love and contentment are considered by the Sufis to be the two highest stations, but their opinions diverge as to which of the two is highest. Different masters speak from different perspectives and all attempts at systematizing the subject inevitably detract something from it, since these states and stations are greatly interdependent and overlapping, each of them able to serve as an opening onto the rest, and each capable of serving as a basis for a particular perspective and method. To give but one example, let us quote this passage from Imām ^{c}Abdallāh al-^{c}Aydarūs's book, *Red Sulphur or the Supreme Elixir*:[12]

> They are consumed with yearning for the flames of Nearness, torn apart with passion, they forsake what is for others habitual, deny their appetites for marriage, food, drink, clothes, houses, riding beasts, and every other kind of worldly thing, as well as socializing with people and the refusal of social eminence which stands as one of the most difficult things. In effect, they reject everything that is not God, making Him their sole quest. They shun sleeping and conversation, their hearts are alight with the fire of love.

In this passage the *shaykh* seems to make love the driving energy behind the spiritual quest from its very beginning, not just one of the two ultimate stations.

In common with all the other stations, the basis of love is knowledge and Imām al-Ḥaddād writes, "Know that the basis of love is knowledge and that its fruit is contemplation. Its lowest degree is that the love of God should be supreme in your heart.... Its uppermost degree is that there remains in your heart not the slightest love for other than God." And when asked which was superior, knowledge or love, he answered that knowledge was more vital and pressing, while love was more noble and subtle. "Love," he said, "is a branch of knowledge and one of its consequences. You cannot love one whom you do not know, but you can know whom you do not love." And he added that "the knowledge that is the consequence of love is indeed knowledge, but they term it contemplation."

The Prophet once said, "Love God for the favors that He grants you, love me for the love of God, and love the people of my house for my love."[13] To love God for His favors and mercies is but the beginning of love, its first rung, yet it is already higher than mere gratitude. To love God because of His beauty and perfection is higher. Higher still is to love Him for no reason other than it being in the nature of things that the relative should be attracted irresistibly toward the Absolute, any lesser degree of attraction being the sign of a flaw or a perversion in its nature which needs to be remedied. To love God is to want to reach Him and this is only feasible through the intermediary of the one capable of showing the way to it, that is the Prophet, may the blessings and peace of God be upon him, and this is why he has said, "None of you believes unless I become dearer to him than his children, his parents, and all other people."[14] As he has also said, "None of you believes unless I am dearer to him than his own self."[15] In practice, to love the Prophet, may God's blessings and peace be upon him, means to emulate him as thoroughly as possible, to remember him constantly with invocations of blessings and peace, and to love his family and mostly those of them who are his true heirs, who carry his knowledge in their hearts and disseminate it across the nation. This is the created being's love for his Creator, but what really matters is whether the Creator loves him. The Imām said, "God has filled my heart with the love of Him. I like the believers solely for their faith and there is no love save for those whom God loves. The servant attains to the love of God only by the regular performance of God's obligatory ordinances together with the supererogatory devotions that move him nearer to Him." The Imām is here referring to the *ḥadith Qudsī* where God says, "My servant draws nearer to me with nothing more pleasing to Me than that which I have made obligatory on him and My servant ceases not to draw nearer to Me with supererogatory devotions until I love him…."[16] And the Imām was once heard saying, "Love has pulverised me, love has smelted me and perfused all my roots, my heart is gone, even though you see me still amongst those people." Such intense love sometimes becomes distressing, and this is suggested by the Imām saying to one of his disciples, "The worries of the world are painful to the people because of their love for it, but, may God be thanked, the love of my Lord (August and Majestic be He) has overflowed upon my heart, which has filled with sorrow and become the house of sorrows." Men of lesser spiritual stature, when subjected to such experiences, are sometimes unable to sustain them. The Imām once predicted that a certain *sayyid* had less than six months to live and, to explain it, said that he "had entered the sea of love abreast and it is slaying him, as for us, we have prepared for it a ship and thus are strong enough for it." Needless to say, the Divine revelations and intimacy that God bestows upon His lovers are also ecstatically pleasurable.

A love of such proportions leaves no room for any created being, not even parents or children. However, those great men's love for their families is observably greater than that of ordinary men and this is because they love them as manifestations of the Divine power and generosity, not for their selves, and this kind of love results in a greater show of affection, greater loyalty, and greater forbearance than most people are ever able to give.

Thus was the Imām inwardly smouldering with love and outwardly serenely attending to the affairs of his family and all other people. That this was his state from an early age is evidenced by his fondness for the poetry of Ibn al-Fāriḍ, the Sultan of Lovers.

As for contentment, the Imām once defines it thus, "According to us contentment is for the heart to remain serene when stricken with afflictions involving people or possessions, or when hardships come, whether they produce fear or want." He writes in *The Book of Assistance,* "You must be content with God's decrees, for this contentment is among the most noble consequences of love and gnosis. It is the attribute of the lover to be pleased with the acts of his Beloved, whether they be sweet or bitter." He then quotes the following *ḥadith*, "When God loves a people He afflicts them; the one who is content receives [His] contentment and the one who is angry receives [His] anger."[17] And in one of his letters, having expressed his deep concern and compassion for the people who had suffered at the hands of one of their rulers, he adds, "the heart swims in an ocean of resignation. The one who forsakes objecting to God, the Exalted (August and Majestic be He) in His decrees and plans, is the one who is blessed and triumphant." The Imām never intended contentment to become sheer passivity and cowardice, however. He acted outwardly with vigor whenever necessary, wrote abrasive letters to the rulers, but remained inwardly serene. To remove another misconception, he wrote the following passage, "Know that supplication, even with insistence, does not compromise contentment, on the contrary, it is part of it. How can it not be when prayer expresses true faith in God's unity, is the language of servitude, and the hallmark of the realization of helplessness, neediness, humility, and poverty? Anyone who has realized these attributes has attained to knowledge, arrival, and the utmost nearness to God."

Sufis often speak of a different category of states such as extinction, absorption, and so on. To distinguish these from the nine stations just described, the Imām writes, "States are of two categories, the first is the one we have just mentioned, the other is that which a heart that is illumined with the lights of self-discipline and effort receives of noble gifts such as intimacy (*uns*), absence (*ghayba*), intoxication (*sukr*), and union (*jam*^{c}). This category of states is not the result of knowledge but that of penetrating concentration in the form of sincere transactions and truthful intentions." In other words they are Divine gifts which may or may not be bestowed upon those who are qualified to receive them, but unlike the other stations of certainty, they do not inevitably follow upon spiritual discipline and effort, neither are they a necessity for the traveler on the path.

Chapter 4
STRUCTURING TIME

Ghazālī on time—invocations and other devotions—teaching sessions—visiting the tomb of Prophet Hūd—social activities and family affairs.

Time is a human being's most precious asset, this is why no man of God ever allows himself to waste it. They count their breaths, not only in the awareness that even in the security and bliss of paradise some will regret every moment that had passed in the world without the remembrance of God, but also because for the elect distraction is deemed a discourtesy punishable by thickening of the veil and an increased remoteness from the Divine Presence. In chapter thirty-eight of *Knowledge and Wisdom*, Imām al-Ḥaddād quotes the following passage from Ghazālī:

> The *Proof of Islam*, may God's mercy be on him, wrote in "Preparing for the Ritual Prayers," a chapter from his book, *The Beginnings of Guidance* (*Bidāyat al-Hidāya*): "You should not neglect your time and use it haphazardly; on the contrary you should bring yourself to account, structure your *awrād* and other functions during each day and night, and assign to each period a fixed specific function. This is how to bring out the *baraka* in each period. But if you leave yourself adrift, wandering aimlessly as cattle do, not knowing how to occupy yourself at every particular moment, your time

> will be lost. This is nothing other than your life, and your life is the capital that you make use of to reach perpetual felicity in the proximity of God the Exalted. Each of your breaths is a priceless jewel, for each of them is irreplaceable and once gone can never be retrieved. Do not be like the deceived fools who are joyous because each day their wealth increases while their life shortens. What good is an increase in wealth when life grows ever shorter? Therefore, be joyous only for an increase in knowledge or good works, for they are your two companions who will accompany you in your grave when your family, wealth, children, and friends stay behind."

Those who accompanied the Imām on his journeys and were intimate enough to be able to observe him closely said that he slept very little, mostly in short snatches, and then so lightly that it was difficult to say whether he was asleep or simply resting. Some nights he slept not at all. He rose long before dawn and began his *awrād* even as he prepared his own coffee. These *awrād* included three *Fātiḥas*, one for the general welfare of all Muslims, a second for his deceased ancestors and teachers, and a third for the fulfillment of his needs and those of the people around him. He also recited *āyat'al-kursī* in a special manner that included the interpolation of one hundred and sixteen invocations of the Divine name *Qawiy* (Mighty) between its words.[18] Having taken his coffee, he made his ritual ablutions with slow deliberation and thoroughness. He then rose to his prayers which he opened with two short *rakᶜas*, followed by the *witr* of eleven very long *rakᶜas*, with prolonged *duᶜā'* in between, and *duᶜā' al-qunūt* at the end. He then carried on with his *awrād* until he heard the *adhān* for the *Fajr* prayer, at which time he prayed the *sunna* at home and waited for the *iqāma* before appearing in the adjoining mosque. He was never known to have prayed the five ritual prayers other than in congregation, at the prime time soon after the *adhān*, and with full attentiveness and reverence. He disliked being spoken to in the interval between the *adhān* and the prayer, since this was the time one is supposed to be collecting oneself, preparing to enter the Divine Presence. He was once heard saying: "We come to prayer in a collected state, with concentration, having become detached from all else." He also said, "Supererogatory prayers were prescribed before the obligatory ones so that the heart may concentrate its attention solely on God, that the prayer may be entered into with presence and concentration."

The mosque and the house of the Imām as they must have looked in his time. A minaret and other buildings were added by his descendants after his death.

Following the *Fajr* prayer he remained seated, reciting his *awrād*, until the sun rose high above the horizon, at which time he prayed the four *rak^{c}as* of *sunnat' al-ishrāq*. Then he continued his *awrād* until it was time for the eight *rak^{c}as* constituting the *sunna* of *Duḥā*. Then he received his guests, had brief teaching sessions, and sometimes listened to Sufi poems being chanted in the Hadrami manner. On Friday he often remained in the mosque until the *jumu^{c}a* prayer, reciting the two *sūras* of al-*kahf* and *Ṭā-hā* among other things. After the *Ẓuhr* prayer and *sunna* he recited one thousand times *lā ilāha illa'allāh*, doubling the number during the month of Ramaḍān and the first five or six days of Shawwāl to bring the total up to seventy thousand, the number said to bring about salvation from the fire of Hell for oneself and for those deceased persons on whose behalf it is done.

The way which leads from the house of the Imām into the courtyard of the mosque.

Most of his regular teaching sessions took place between ᶜ*Aṣr* and *Maghrib*, following which he prayed the twenty *rakᶜas* called *ṣalāt'al-awwābīn*. His sessions of *dhikr* took place after ᶜ*Ishā'*. He retired to his quarters to continue with his *awrād.* These he preferred to keep hidden, except from those of his family and disciples he hoped would emulate him.

Once he had become a renowned master and his free time severely curtailed, his visits to his ancestors and masters at the cemetery became restricted to Fridays and Tuesdays after ᶜ*Aṣr*, and he was always accompanied by a large crowd. These were occasions for reflecting on death and the grave and one's condition following departure from this world, for remembering one's ancestors and spiritual masters and offering Qur'ānic recitations, invocations, and *duᶜā'* (supplications) for them, and praying for oneself and one's loved ones.

The Imām also visited the tomb of the Prophet Hūd, may peace be upon him, which is situated at three day's traveling distance from Tarīm. He made thirty such visits, usually stopping at the town of ᶜĪnāt to visit the great Shaykh Abū Bakr ibn Sālim and the other saints in his vicinity. The visits took place in the month of Shaᶜbān, from the twelfth until the sun set on the fourteenth. Again, he was always accompanied by a large number of relatives, disciples, and visitors. During these three days, they read the *mawlid* of the Prophet, may God's blessings and peace be upon him, and held sessions of *dhikr* and *duᶜā'*. He liked everyone to stay the full three days, for this had been the pattern established by their ancestors, and such things he always took very seriously. He was once heard saying, "The one who leaves, his visit is null, since he has not conformed to the arrangements made by the *sayyids*, that which they have made a custom. It is as if he were opposing them. Shaykh Abū-Bakr ibn Sālim only established the *ḥaḍra* so that the people may gather for a time remembering God, making *du^{c}ā'*, and reading the *mawlid* in order that by such a gathering the *baraka* should occur. The one who departs early after attending the *ḥaḍra* earns half a visit, while the one who departs [at the end] earns a full visit. It may be that there are Divine matters depending on the arrangements of the *sayyids*."

The Valley of Hūd

At his quarters and mosque at al-Ḥāwī the stream of visitors was uninterrupted. Some came out of curiosity to see how this famous person looked and behaved, others were in need of social or financial support, intercession near the authorities, or counseling regarding their worldly affairs. There were also those who sought religious knowledge and those who were in pursuit of things spiritual. He received them all affably, inquired about their names, those of their fathers and tribes, and what the current situation was in their home town. None left his presence feeling that he had received less than a full share of his attention.

He always gave his family ample time, never allowing his other obligations to interfere with his personal life. He was extremely affectionate with his children and grandchildren whom he raised in his own mold. His daughters-in-law brought their problems to him rather than to their own parents.

In the summertime, the Imām liked to go out to the countryside riding on his mare, led by a servant, and spend a day or two in rural surroundings.

The grave and dome of Prophet Hūd
and stairway leading up to it.

Chapter 5
THE SUFI

What is Sufism? Who is the Sufi? Union and separation—the five investitures of taqwā—the different aspects of the Sufi.

Sufism is the *tawḥīd* of the elect, the path to the Ultimate Reality, the journey from the accidental to the essential, from the illusory to the Real, from the relative to the Absolute. It is the effort to reach the reality of *tawḥīd* by the methodical application of the science of the ego, the science of the ailments and the veils of the heart with their remedies, the science of the degrees of the soul with the requirements of each degree, spiritual station, and state.

The term 'Sufi,' often used abusively for anyone connected in any way to Sufism, is usually used by the Sufis themselves to designate he who has arrived, that is attained to the direct experience of the Absolute, and who thus sees nothing but God and desires nothing but God. Speaking out of personal experience, the Imām wrote, "The man who has arrived is a servant who has reached a level, in his knowledge of God, which marks the limit of that which men can know about Him. Those in this degree differ to an incalculable extent; they are in either one of two states, one of which is called union (*jamᶜ*), and the other separation (*farq*). When the state of union comes upon such a man he becomes extinct as regards [his awareness of] himself and others, and is absorbed in his Lord, [to the extent of being] totally annihilated in him. At such a time no thoughts occur to him and he perceives nothing that exists, save the One whose existence is real, Majestic and High is He." In the same letter he adds, "Gnostics yearn for union, but the Real, mercifully moves them out from this, that they may discharge their obligations and that their bodies may not waste and their bones wither away." The union meant here is not to be confused with that designated in Arabic by the word *ittiḥād*, since the latter signifies union between two separate entities, which, when used in this context, amounts to nothing short of polytheism. This possibility is clearly negated by the affirmation of Divine Transcendence, which concludes the Imām's first quoted sentence, "Majestic and High is He." The union alluded to by the Sufis is the state where the servant ceases to be aware of his individual "I", thus freeing his heart for the awareness of the One Reality, which he can evidently never hope to either exhaust or encompass. Similarly, the state of separation or subsistence, which is subsequent to union or extinction, is not the return to the previous separative experience of the "I", but to a state where one is "neither veiled from the Real by creation, nor from creation by the Real." It is to remain in the Unitary Presence, while simultaneously attending to one's familial, social, and other duties. This is the *tamkīn* or mastery of the elect, and it is this mastery, which is a God-given grace, that allows them to function as scholars, teachers, judges, spiritual guides, and so on, whereas a man overwhelmed by the contemplation of the Divine Lights is hardly able to do so. On the other hand, the traveler (*sālik*) or seeker (*murīd*) who has yet to arrive is not called a Sufi but a *mutaṣawwif*, which means one who is affiliated to and emulating the Sufis. Seekers vary in their natural aptitudes and determination to reach the goal. A true seeker, as the Imām explains in *Good Manners of the Spiritual Disciple* is "one who is enslaved neither by other than God nor by forms, who is neither vanquished by his appetites nor dominated by his habits", and "he is intensely striving to draw nearer to his Lord, disdainful of the world, and never repeats his errors." The method used by such travelers in their striving is designated in Arabic by the term *ṭarīqa* which is the practice of *sharīᶜa* in depth and to the full, that is with utter sincerity and fervor.

The foundation of all this is *taqwā*, the fear of God, or constant awareness of Divine Omniscience. *Taqwā* exists to some extent in all Muslims, however it is only to be witnessed in its pure form in the elect, the *awliyā'*. The Prophet, may God's blessings and peace be upon him, was once asked, "O Messenger of God, who is the most honorable of men?" His reply was, "He who possesses the most *taqwā*."[19] In his *Book of Mutual Reminding*, the Imām quotes a long passage from Imām al-Ghazālī where the different levels of *taqwā* are described, the first being fear of God and awe, followed by compliance with His injunctions and worshipping Him, then by the purification of the heart through what is known by the Sufis as the 'battle with the ego", (*jihād al-nafs*).

Imām ᶜAbdallāh al-ᶜAydarūs wrote that *taqwā*, when true, brings on five investitures, or five Divine gifts. The first concerns the body and the observance by the physical form of the legal prescriptions. The second concerns the heart, here taken to mean the soul, and is the realization of the stations of certainty. These stations result from conscious effort (*jihād*) and self discipline (*riyāḍa*). These changes were more than once likened by Imām al-Ḥaddād to alchemy. He once said: "The intention of the virtuous in their self disciplining practices is but to conquer their egos and slay them. When this happens they come upon the Supreme Elixir, for in this context, it [the ego] is the greatest opponent and the matter can never be completed until it is slain. In this respect it is like the alchemical mercury which has to be killed in order to achieve the purpose from it; and to kill either of them is difficult, yet the purpose from each is never obtained until after their death." He also said, "The people of this time seldom fulfill all the conditions. Whenever most conditions are fulfilled, there is always one that is missing, so that the rest is of no use and the goal is not reached, just as in alchemy, when you perform every step correctly except one, the reaction stops. Alchemy is either that God grants a man detachment so that gold and dust become equal to him, or that He provides him with the minimum sustenance and keeps him occupied with devotions."

Bayt al-Ḥadra, the renovated old house of the Imām in the town center where he used to hold his session of *dhikr* after *Jumu*[c]*a*.

Spiritual alchemy, that Ghazālī called, "The Alchemy of Happiness," is that which leads to gnosis. The Imām very succinctly defines it thus: "Alchemy is '*Say: He, God, is One*', the important thing is purity of the heart and the meeting of spirits."

To return to the stations of virtue, once these are realized they are permanent acquisitions, and once mastered they open the way for the spiritual states to occur. Again according to al-ᶜAydarūs, these states are those of love, yearning, awe, intimacy, contentment, gratitude, nearness, arrival, extinction, and subsistence. These are the third investiture, that which concerns the spirit. They are transitory states that occur by Divine grace and not by effort. The fourth concerns the secret (*sirr*) and is the reality of *tawḥīd* or unification. The man invested with these four Divine gifts becomes perfect in *sharīᶜa*, *ṭarīqa*, and *ḥaqīqa*, and is but one step removed from the fifth or ultimate investiture which is the secret of *khilāfa* or viceregency.

It is perhaps necessary to reiterate at this point that Sufism is the active and methodical traveling of the spiritual path and only those who do so deserve to be called Sufis. There are other categories of saints who receive their Openings as a purely gratuitous Divine grace, without prior methodic preparation, a rare but well-known phenomenon. Most of these are *majdhūbs* or ecstatics, they are undoubtedly gnostics, but cannot be called Sufis.

The Sufi then is the man who has reached the summit of spiritual achievement. He is by definition a saint and a gnostic. He may or may not have an outward function such as that of scholar or spiritual guide, and he may or may not have a hidden function such as that of the *abdāl* (substitutes), or *aqṭāb* (poles). These are integrated aspects of the same being, yet, in order to comprehend them to the extent possible to outside observers, we shall devote a separate chapter to each of them, beginning with the two inward facets, sanctity and gnosis, then the two outward functions, namely those of leading scholar and spiritual master, and finally the hidden function, that of Pole or *Quṭb*, which is that of the supreme leader of the Circle of Sainthood.

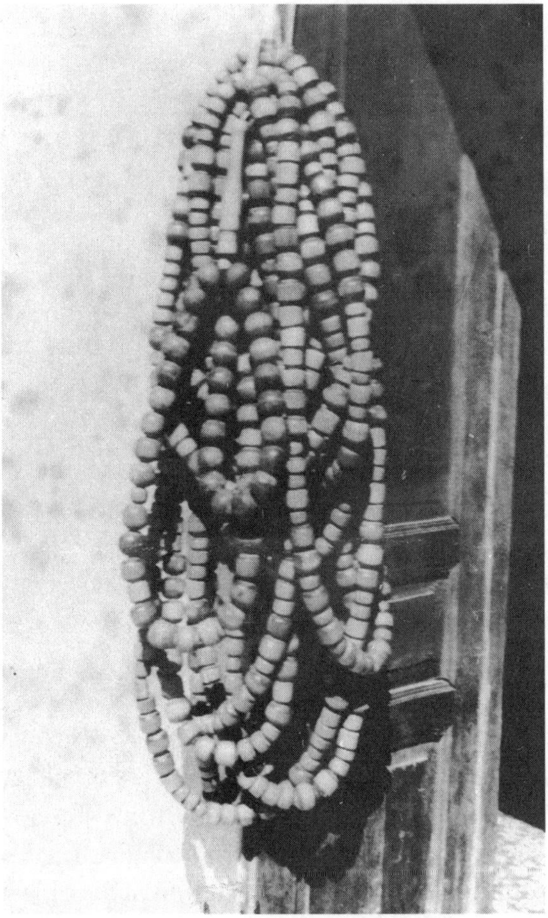

The rosary of one thousand beads which belonged to the Imām.

Chapter 6
THE SAINT

What is sanctity? The Imām's behavior toward his guests—fluctuation of spiritual states between majesty and beauty—Divine protection of saints—the baraka of the Imām—powerlessness before Divine omnipotence—the lights of sanctity—dealings with the jinn.

"I bear witness," said Sayyid Aḥmad ibn Hāshim al Ḥabashī, "that Sayyidī ᶜAbdallāh is a spiritual being in whom no trace of humanity remains." This degree of spirituality is that where nothing remains of the passionate ego, it having given place to the Divine Attributes, which, when manifested to the full in a human being, are seen outwardly as the perfection of virtue. It was to the same *sayyid* that the Imām once wrote, "God has servants whom He has so occupied with Himself that they attend to nothing else. He causes them to become unaware of their own selves, so that they see only Him. He is their intimate comfort in their retreats and their companion hour after hour. Their bodies are active in His obedience, their secrets are unaware of all else, their intellects received from Him, the immediate world distracts them not from the invisible world-to-come. They know the purpose for which they were created and are therefore resolute. They know the exaltation of the object of their quest and are therefore eager and determined to reach it. They perceive the villainy of this world and therefore turn and walk away from it. *"These are God's party, surely it is God's party who are the successful."* [58:22] God's party are the *awliyā'*, the saints. The rendering of the Arabic term *walī* as saint is not wholly satisfactory. A *walī* is a friend or ally of God, a man who has surrendered himself totally to God so that he has become, in return, constantly enveloped in Divine solicitude. The term is sometimes used to designate the highest degree of sanctity where the saint becomes a Sufi and a gnostic. "The *walī*," says al-ᶜAydarūs, "is someone who has mastered the station of *taqwā*, which is the foundation of everything else, then the ten stations, then the spiritual states have come to him, then he was given the opening of gnosis, which is the eye, followed by the truth of certainty." However, the term is also frequently used in a broader sense to indicate the aspect of saintliness that precedes and is a prerequisite to gnosis, saintliness having more to do with the perfection of virtue, while gnosis is knowledge. One may thus be a saint but not necessarily a gnostic yet. This recalls the old debate, does a saint know that he is one? The answer is that some do and some do not. Those who receive the Major Opening (*al-fatḥ al-kabīr*) are in no doubt concerning their spiritual status, whereas those who do not can never be certain, despite the numerous extrinsic signs that they may experience. Their Opening is held in store for them, they receive it as soon as they depart from this world and enter the *barzakh*.

The Imām's sanctity was recognized by most everyone who had an interest in such matters and people came to him for all kinds of reasons, some worldly, some other worldly. He received them all gracefully, smiled and talked to each according to his level of understanding, never allowing them to drift into trivial conversation in his presence, leaving each of them satisfied that he had received his undivided attention. He gave them his time, his possessions, and his knowledge, yet he longed to be alone with his Lord. "I wish I were in the wilderness," he once said, "delighting in communing with God the Exalted and finding my intimate comfort in Him, Transcendent be He, with none other than He seeing me." Then, with some of the functions that he had been invested with in mind, he added, "Were God ever to will this to happen, He would raise those who would undertake the dissemination of knowledge and the provision of hospitality for the guests, for these two things I cannot abandon." Indeed, he nearly always had guests in his house. Some came for a day or part of a day, others for longer periods. Some expected assistance, financial or otherwise, others brought gifts that he accepted, in compliance with the *sunna*, then gave away, also in accordance with the *sunna*. He received them sitting on the floor, dignified and serene, either cross-legged or with his right knee held upright and his right hand resting on it. He was awe inspiring, not because of anything that he said or did, but because of the spiritual power emanating from him. He was aware of this, despite his blindness, and was heard commenting on it thus: "God, August and Majestic is He, clothes us with awesome dignity, for in reality, we are people of beauty." Meaning that his outward form sometimes manifested the Divine aspect of Majesty, while his heart received the effulgence of the Divine Aspect of Beauty. Indeed, he was described by one of his disciples as "Always smiling, basking in the lights of the Holiest Beauty which he was beholding; his joy and delight communicating themselves to his companions, so much so that those who sat with him forgot their pains, sicknesses, problems, hunger and thirst, wishing only that the session should last forever." This interplay of majesty and beauty is frequently to be observed in great men of

Prayer cap of the Imām preserved by sewing green silk around the edge.

Miḥrāb of the Imām in the room adjoining the mosque on the ground floor of his house. This was his place of *khalwa*.

God, particularly the people of *tamkīn*, the firmly established masters. Others fluctuate between these two states, and others still are dominated by one of them. This state of the Imām explains why he was able to affirm that "No person who sat with me ever distracted me from the remembrance of God." Since it is often said that the remembrance of the gnostics is contemplation, and indeed the station of subsistence is that where the servant is neither veiled by creation from contemplating the Real, nor by this contemplation from attending to creation.

Being the locus upon which descends the Divine effulgence of grace implies two important things. The first is that the saint is surrounded by a barrier of Divine protection and solicitude, which effectively extends to include his family, disciples, neighbors, and others who are attached to him. In 1071 H. the Imām gave indications in one of his poems that his descendants and everyone attached to him, till the Day of Reckoning, were under Divine protection. The second is that it is through him that this Divine grace reaches the community. The first of these explains why those who behaved with hostility toward the Imām were treated harshly by heaven on many occasions, despite his having forgiven them. It is an integral part of sanctity not to be vindictive, to perceive both good and evil as coming from God, thus never wasting time in pointing accusing fingers here and there. In effect, the Imām was well known to endure quite patiently whatever harm came to him from his relatives, in-laws, companions, visitors, or any other member of the community. This had always been and still is the ᶜAlawī tradition. His rule was, as he put it, "We never censure or ask to account those who are neglectful towards us." When one of his companions complained to him that a certain man had abused him, he answered, "Can you not bear a few words? We hear what is being said to us, forgive those who abuse us, and treat them well." And when a man publicly abused him on the street, he sent him a gift of money and apologized to him. God, however, does not let the offender go unpunished, as He says in a *ḥadith qudsī*: "He who injures a *walī* of Mine, I declare war on him."[20] And this Divine law took its toll on the Imām's adversaries, so much so that he used to say, "We have observed that those who either cause us harm or treat us discourteously are swiftly chastised and not granted a respite. Because of this we sometimes speak to them in a somewhat reproachful manner, that their chastisement not be hastened, out of mercy and pity for them."

He once again endured silently a man's injury, and then forgave him as was his custom. Nevertheless, the man fell prey to a severe illness that afflicted him for a long time and of which he eventually died. Someone insinuated in the Imām's presence that it had been caused by his *duᶜā'*, which he immediately denied saying that, "We never make *duᶜā'* against a Muslim, but God, August and Majestic is He, is jealous for His saints when they are harmed." Having said that, he rose to his feet and made for the mosque, where he attended the man's funeral prayer, prayed for him, remaining with them until the burial was completed.

This by no means implies that neither hardships nor sufferings befell the Imām and the people around him. For after all, the Prophet, may blessings and peace be upon him, had clearly stated that those most afflicted with hardships were the Prophets, then the next in rank, then the next, and so on.[21] What this means is that that which is most important, namely one's faith, comes first under this Divine protection, then the saint's pleas are more often than not accepted by God, so that the hardships that are on the point of striking are either arrested altogether, or lightened.[22] The saint may also be allowed to intervene, using his spiritual powers, in some difficult situations. This subject will be dealt with more fully later in the work.

As for the diffusion of the Divine grants, the Imām once said: "Were all the people of this age, old and young, male and female, to come to us, they would all benefit, both in their religious and worldly affairs, their outwards and their inwards, in the immediate and remote future. There are people whose bodies are in the Maghrib and whose spirits are here with us, and there are others whose condition is the opposite of this."

The *baraka* of the Imām had a penetrating radiance to it and was eagerly sought by the people. He often told them: "We have put the *madad* (spiritual secret of blessings and assistance) in our food and water," implying that, in addition to the *baraka* that one normally expects in the food of saints, there was a particular secret in his. This was also an encouragement for his guests to eat as much as they possibly could, for "those who desire much *madad* should eat much." This characteristic still runs in the house of al-Ḥaddād. Visitors to their houses who know about this make sure to eat only after having formed the intention to receive the *madad* of al-Ḥaddād, some go so far as to make a specific request with each mouthful. This is identical with the secret of the well of Zamzam, the water of which we are urged to drink in as large a quantity as possible, while petitioning God for all our needs. "The water of Zamzam," said the Prophet, may God's blessings and peace be upon him, "is for whatever it is drunk for."[23] And indeed the Imām explicitly confirmed the resemblance thus; "The one who drinks a draught of our water is as one who has drunk from Zamzam." This resemblance was one aspect of the Prophetic heritage that Imām al-Ḥaddād had received. To prepare him to receive the more inward aspects of this heritage, another event took place that had its prototype in the *sunna*. "My breast was split open in the mosque of Banī ᶜAlawī," said he, not elaborating further, since no Muslim would fail to recognize this event for what it was—a Divinely ordained purification of the heart modeled on that to which the Prophet was subject in Makka. Such graces are granted by right to Prophets, but only by refraction to their heirs.

The Prophet, may God's blessings and peace be upon him, often informed his Companions of his special attributes. These attributes were those specifically which they needed to know in order to be able to act upon such knowledge, rather than those which were secrets between him and his Lord. He informed them for instance that he would intercede on their behalf on Judgment Day, that after his death he would be aware of their actions so that he would "thank God when what he saw was good and ask Him to forgive when it was otherwise."[24] He also stated that he was "the Master of the Children of Adam," adding "and this is not to boast."[25] That is, it was not pride that drove him to make this statement, and neither did he feel proud having made it. Similarly, there was never pride in Imām al-Ḥaddād's heart when he said, "We envy the Prophet's Companions solely for his company; had we lived in his time, we would have been among their foremost." Now the Muslim nation has always held by consensus that the Companions are never to be equalled, the least among them ranking higher than the highest of later saints. The Imām's statement should therefore be taken to mean that if you put aside their most important attribute, which is their having physically kept company with the Prophet, then he was a spiritual match for them. This amounted to an invitation to the people to come to him, since keeping his company would profit them spiritually nearly as much as if they had kept the company of one of the Companions. Sayyid ʿUmar al-ʿAṭṭās once said, "Sayyid ʿAbdallāh is a robe which had lain folded up until it was spread in these times, for he belongs to the seventh or fourth centuries, but God delayed him for the felicity of the people of his time." These words were heard by ʿAbdal-Raḥmān Ba-Sharāḥīl and reported to the Imām who said: "O ʿAbdal-Raḥmān, I, may God be praised, do not belong to the people of this time, though God has placed me among them. I am alone, separated from them in my heart." Thirty years later he was to say, "I am not one of the people of this time, I am one of those of the second generation, and were it not for the [obligation to maintain] courtesy with the first generation, I would have said I am one of them, for they were none other than the Companions, may God be pleased with them. Look at my state and that of the people of the time. Do I resemble them or do they resemble me?" "The saint is a sign of God," he also said, trying to explain the nature of saints to the people, "and I am a sign of God, but my soul is part of creation, and this is a testimony that you can meet your Lord with on the Day of Arising." He also said, "We are as the sun for the people, those who open their doors will receive as much of it as they allow their doors to let in," and, "We are the kings of both earth and heaven."

Yet despite these and similar declarations, those who knew him found him exceedingly humble, fearful of his Lord, and one who treated the least of people on equal terms. "Our way," he said, "is to meet God with utmost poverty and not give any consideration to [secondary] causes." Which meant that he was aware of his total powerlessness before the Divine will and power, and, attributing all his good actions and devotional activities to Divine grace, he could only meet his Lord in a state of total destitution. And in effect, he once wrote to Sayyid ^{c}Alī al-^{c}Aydarūs, “Pray for your brother who is destitute of everything except his hope in God’s forgiveness and the strength of his desire for his hidden mercies and His gracious covering of his shortcomings in fulfilling His rights to the limit and the end.” To speak of “the limit and the end” is characteristic of the Imām, whose limits, although far beyond those of the highest gnostics of his time, were still perceived by him as inadequate. He spoke of himself thus: “We are weak and destitute, we cannot bear an atom of hardship, nor can we sustain it; God’s safeguard is a better protection for us, a better cover for our weaknesses, and is more appropriate for our servitude and poverty.” He taught others never to “ascribe any worth to the one who believes himself to be worthy,” and “the one who says ‘I am qualified,’ even if he is so. He is told, ‘you are not qualified.’ The one who says, ‘I am not qualified,’ even if he should be as he says is told, ‘you are qualified.’ The ways of the inward are different from those of the outward.” Then he quoted the story of the man who was a contemporary of Shaykh ^{c}Abdal-Qādir and, hearing his praises, said, “I have seen nothing of Shaykh ^{c}Abdal-Qādir in the *Malakūt*, and [you can] go and tell him this!” To which the *shaykh* replied. “You enter [the *Malakūt*] from the lowest level while I am in the highest, so you see me not.” Then the *shaykh* provided as proof of his contention a specific event that had happened inwardly to that man, adding that it was only through his mediation that it had happened.

The Imām once made the very pertinent remark that, “Each man of God sees what he is granted as immense, but seldom sees what the others are granted.” And to understand this point is vital if one is to place in proper perspective much of what great men have said concerning the special gifts bestowed upon them. Similarly, one should understand these same men's confessions of their sins and shortcomings in the light of the following statement by the Imām: "Know that such a *wilāya* is an immense thing and that its possessor never indulges in permissible and pleasurable things, let alone minor sins." Prophets are infallible, whereas saints who are established in that station where they are uninterruptedly in the Prophet's presence are said to be "guarded." They are thus separated by invisible barriers from the very possibility of sin and, as says the Imām, "their utterances where they confess their shortcomings, their humility before their Lord, and the unworthiness of their ranks in relation to the [exaltation of] their contemplation" are not in reality sins, since they concern nothing other than what they perceive as imperfection in their acts of obedience.

Another attribute of Prophets and saints is their being surrounded by scores of angels, filling the space around them with light, in addition to the inward light which is sometimes visible from the exterior. The Companions have described how the Prophet's face shone more brightly than the full moon, and how by that light the lady ᶜĀ'isha was able to see a needle that had fallen to the ground on a moonless night. Imām al-Ḥaddād said that when Moses, may peace be upon him, returned from the mountain, he had to veil his face to hide the light that shone from it. He added that this had also been the station of Sayyid Aḥmad al-Badawī and Shaykh Abū-Yaᶜzā of Morocco, Abū Madian's *shaykh*. It is well known that al-Badawī wore a double veil to hide the light that shone forth from his face, so blinding to the onlooker it was. As for Imām al-Ḥaddād, this was not his state, his lights were only seen by those with some spirituality, each according to the strength of his inner eye. He consciously concealed his state from the common people saying, "The people are veiled from us by two thick veils, one is from us and it is that we neither want them nor wish to be known to them; the other is from them, it is their lack of desire for goodness." Thus, despite the fact that his fame spread to the four corners of the land, he still maintained that had he wished it to spread further he would have eclipsed everyone else.

Apart from the angels, the Imām had dealings with the jinn. He was aware that they attended his teaching sessions and often told his disciples that some of his statements which they could not easily understand were meant for another audience. "When we speak in the course of a session," he said, "let no one think that he is particularly meant by what we say, rather is destined generally for all who hear it. When we speak in a session and those present understand and apply what we have said it will be evidence in their favor, otherwise there are others who hear and do not see. Our speech is by Divine order." And Sayyid Muḥammad ibn Shaykh al-Jufrī said he once saw a viper coiled besides the Imām during the afternoon teaching session; a man reaching for a stick to kill it with was sharply stopped by the Imām, "Don't kill the viper, leave her be!" She thus remained in her place until the end of the session and, when the Imām had terminated his *duʿā'* and *Fātiḥa*, quietly departed. The Imām also stated that the jinn in the town of al-Hajarayn had offered to place themselves in his service but that he had declined their offer.

Chapter 7
THE GNOSTIC

What is gnosis? Stages of gnosis: from perception of created beings, to that of the Divine acts, attributes, and essence—certainty: knowledge, eye, and truth of certainty—unveiling—contemplation—ascension.

The Imām said, "Our knowledge is the knowledge of al-Junayd, the Master of the Group, who [locked his door and] placed the key under his thigh whenever he wished to discourse on it for the benefit of his close disciples. As for the sciences that we have taken upon ourselves to teach, they are the function of the exoterist scholar, but they have shunned them and we feared lest they become extinct." He also said, "We have found knowledge, not by means of words and phrases, nor by jostling with other men, but by a heart freed from the world, by weeping in the deep of the night, and constant vigilance for the Almighty." This knowledge is none other than *ma^{c}rifa*, gnosis, the aim of every traveler, the direct experiential knowledge of God, the contemplative vision of the Divine Acts and attributes, and beyond them the unitive experience of the Divine Essence.

According to the Sufis, the Divine Essence is veiled by the Attributes, these are veiled by the Acts, which are in turn veiled by the created forms. Those for whom the Acts are unveiled when the veil of manifested forms is lifted, are ushered into the station of reliance. Those for whom the

Attributes are unveiled when the veil of the Acts is lifted, become contented and resigned. As for those before whom the Essence is unveiled when the veil of the Attributes is lifted, they become extinct in unity. Thus, the realization of the *tawḥīd* of the Acts precedes that of the Attributes, which in turn precedes that of the Essence. Within each stage there are innumerable degrees, and variations. This is gnosis proper. However, the traveler's opening may also involve created beings. Anything from the seventh heaven down to the lowest material level may be unveiled before him. Let us here recall the "inspired knowledge" of Sayyidunā al-Khidr, as the Qur'ān states, *"One of Our servants to whom We had given mercy from Us, and We had taught him knowledge proceedings from Us,"* [18:65]. This knowledge proceeding directly from God or *ᶜilm ladunnī*, concerned the affairs of a ship and its poor owners, a young boy and his parents, and two orphans and their treasure. This would have been the lowest degree of unveiling, that of the material world, had it not been for the fact that al-Khidr not only had a clear vision of each situation, but also received his instructions directly from Heaven. This degree of unveiling is given to those who are entrusted with hidden functions in order to enable them to carry them out. The spiritual stature of al-Khidr is of course immensely greater than this, but he was given in the Qur'ān as an example of those servants of God whose actions in the world are strictly according to Divine instructions. *"I did it not of my own bidding,"* said al-Khidr [18:82].

Knowledge (*maᶜrifa*) has traditionally been divided into three levels: intellectual knowledge, eye or vision, and truth of certainty. The first of these is already certainty and therefore firmly transcends not only conjecture, but also conviction. It does not depend upon proofs and logical arguments, although still capable of being strengthened by them. Certainty gives the human intelligence an extra dimension, since it allows it to perceive Divine signs both in the created forms and in the Qur'ān, while accepting them as such. This level belongs to all Muslims, varying greatly from one individual to another in breadth as well as in depth. Its higher reaches are what the Sufis call *muḥādara*, or "imposed awareness." Here, Divine solicitude imposes on the servant's awareness the constant presence of the higher worlds and the perception of signs as signs, forcing him to take heed. Sufis prepare for this *muḥādara* by constant *dhikr*. Then the seeker begins to have flashes of unveiling, eventually leading him into the next level which is that of the eye or vision of certainty.

This is the stage when *mukāshafa* or unveiling begins. It involves essentially the Divine Acts and Attributes, but also any degree or degrees of the created worlds. Here logical operations and proofs are entirely discarded. Some of these degrees were alluded to by Imām al-Ḥaddād in the following words: "When a man rises above the dense veils of both ego and body by effort and self-discipline, he knows more and more, until he may hear at one stage the 'turning of the spheres,' and this is so intensely pleasurable that it may absorb him completely and abolish his earthly appetites. This is the pleasure of the spirit from which man is veiled by his physical appetites. When he reaches things in the Divine Order his pleasure and absorption are immeasurably more than those produced by the 'spheres.' God raised the Prophet and gradually unveiled before him all the degrees of existence, until He made him reach the level where He spoke to him face to face. So it was with Abraham when he 'saw' the planets, then the moon, then the sun, then turned to the Divine Presence."

There are allusions to his visions of the higher worlds in the *Dīwān* and his collected sayings. Speaking of the World of the Command, "*ᶜĀlam al amr* is the spiritual world," he once said; "It is too subtle to be grasped by either the senses or the mind."

The *ḥadith Qudsī* states: "My servant ceases not to draw nearer to me with supererogatory devotions until I love him. When I do I become his hearing wherewith he hears and his sight wherewith he sees…."[26] This spiritual sight is able to penetrate all the created worlds and reach beyond the Guarded Tablet to the Divine Decrees. Sayyid al-Hunduwān said, "Sayyid ᶜAbdallāh beholds, by means of unveiling, the definitive decrees, which are unalterable. Therefore, whatever he chooses to inform about inevitably comes true. On the other hand, the saints of his time behold only the level of "erasure and confirmation."[27] Erasure and confirmation pertain to the level of the Guarded Tablet, the decrees inscribed on it being capable of being erased, altered, or carried out, according to God's final will. Again, by means of the spiritual power of hearing mentioned in the *ḥadith,* gnostics hear the Divine address in the last third of the night when, as the Prophet, may God's blessings and peace be upon him, has informed us, God "descends to the Terrestrial Heaven", to dispense His forgiveness and favors to those who are awake remembering Him.[28]

The culmination of unveiling is *mushāhada* or contemplation. This is the knowledge of extinction where the Absolute is alone present and the subjective awareness of the relative disappears. Beyond that is subsistence. The Imām once said that the unveiling of the Divine Attributes "abolishes the servant's power of discrimination, rendering him unaware of himself and of his own human nature." This is a state which the traveler experiences for a time, then it departs and "when obligatory devotions such as prayers and fasts are missed due to such state of absorption, they must be requitted subsequently (*qaḍā'*)." As for the master, "some of these realities become permanently unveiled for him, others are veiled at times and unveiled at others. Such a man attends to his daily life, engages in earning and industry, and these neither harm nor veil him from his Lord."

When Sufis say that "The heart of the believer is the Throne of the all Merciful," they evidently mean by 'believer' the perfect servant whose heart is free from everything that is not God. Imām al-Ḥaddād was once heard to describe his *shaykh* ᶜUmar al-ᶜAṭṭās as, "a heart and a lord," (*qalb wa rabb*).

The level of the eye or vision of certainty belongs to the elect and that of the truth of certainty to the elect of the elect.

A famous Sufi once said that he and his peers are often taken up in spirit to the Terrestrial Heaven, or the second or third, each according to his allotted share; and some are taken up to the Lote tree of the Limit and there God speaks to them. In the same vein al-Faqīh al-Muqaddam once said that he had been raised up to the Lote Tree seven times. As for Imām al-Ḥaddād, he said, "A saint is granted (part of) that which a Prophet is granted. The *miᶜrāj* was erected before me in the al-Hujayra mosque and I was taken up to heaven and came into the presence of God." This is not to be taken to mean that the *miᶜrāj* of the Imām, or any other saint for that matter, is identical with that of the Prophet, but only that they follow the same pattern, each according to the rank assigned to him by Divine solicitude. This ascent implies the acquisition of higher knowledge, and indeed the Imām states that he had been granted the science of the Name as a grace, that for each letter in the *Fātiḥa* he had been given numerous sciences, that the knowledge of the Qur'ān had been unlocked for him, and that "were the people of this time to accept with fairness the knowledge that I possess, I would have written many books on the meaning of a single verse in God's Book. There comes to my heart sciences for which I find no recipient." And, "We have been given seventy sciences concerning the verse, '*Our Lord, give us in this world what is good and in the next world what is good*,' [2:201]. Referring to the Qur'ān in one of his letters he said, "There is no secret in the *Mulk* or the *Malakūt* but that it has been deposited in it. Only those may reach its secrets and exalted meanings, however, who have purified themselves from committing sins, harboring wishes or desires which drive the heart toward enjoying worldly things, adorned their inwards and outwards with behavior and attributes that are worthy, and concentrated on their Lord by abandoning all else, all created beings, whether they be exalted or low. And he whom God guides, he is the rightly guided one." In a letter written to Shaykh Bā-Faḍl after his return from *ḥajj* the Imām reveals that his knowledge is derived from the supreme source that he designates as "the mystery of mysteries, the unfathomable depth of the Divine Presence."

It is impossible for those who have not experienced or, as Sufis would say, "tasted" such things to grasp what gnosis is. It is also impossible for those still struggling somewhere along the path to understand the nature of the knowledge of such giants as Imām al-Ḥaddād. The difficulty in the verbal transmission of gnosis is twofold. Firstly, much of this kind of knowledge is inexpressible and this is why masters use symbols, metaphors, and subtle indications. He wrote to one of his disciples: "Praise belongs to God, the praise of one who has beheld and observed, and his tongue has expressed some of that which his heart has beheld, but he was powerless before the reality of what had been unveiled to him, and the limits of language were too narrow to describe it." He also wrote in another letter: "Praise belongs to God, Who has illumined the heart of His saints with the lights of His nearness and graces, and delighted their spirits with the bliss of His intimacy and communion, and honored them with the contemplation of the holiness of His Beauty and Majesty." To comment on such a passage adequately would require a whole volume. Secondly, the recipient must be highly qualified and such people have always been rare. This is why, despite the multitude of great saints and gnostics among the Imām's contemporaries and disciples, he still said: "We possess sciences for which we can find no recipient. Our likeness is that of a merchant who sailed into a port carrying goods in abundance. The townsmen came to buy from him and he showed them first of all the tissues of the lowest quality. They proved unwilling to offer a fair price for them, seeing that, he abstained from showing them the higher quality ones." And he once remarked that this was part of the heritage he had received from Imām ᶜAlī, his ancestor, who was the repository of the Prophetic higher knowledge, and who sometimes became so full with it that he breathed it into a well when unable to dispense it to anyone.

To express that which is capable of being expressed, the art of the masters consists in using the language of the Qur'ān and *ḥadith* so as not to unsettle their listeners and arouse confusion. Conformity with the exoteric aspect of religious sciences is greatly encouraged and extravagant utterances discouraged even though they may be true in essence. "The sciences of unveiling," said the Imām, "do not contradict the sciences of transaction. The meanings are correct but the [forms] differ with the [differences in] self-discipline." This statement means that each man expresses the same reality from his own particular perspective and the level corresponding to his self-disciplining method and intensity of effort. Descriptions may thus vary. However, scholars of authority are all agreed that whenever there is a seeming contradiction between the letter of the *sharīᶜa* and what is perceived by means of unveiling the safer course lies in adhering to *sharīᶜa,* since this is where the divine guarantee of inerrancey lies, not in unveiling.

Chapter 8
THE SPIRITUAL MASTER

Who is the spiritual master? Functions of the master—the two methods, that of the Drawn Near and that of the People of the Right Hand—spiritual transmission—protection of the disciple by the master—circumspection—reticence to reveal the secrets of the unseen—attitude toward ibn ᶜArabī and ibn al-Fāriḍ—dangers of the path—influence of the Imām in other countries.

The spiritual master is he whom God entrusts with the means to both guide and assist the seeker on his inner journey. Guidance pertains to the outward domain and depends on knowledge and experience, while assistance is inward and depends on the *shaykh's* spiritual power and the magnitude of his Opening. Ideally, the *shaykh* should be someone who has received the "Major Opening," so that nothing of the disciple remains hidden from him. He is the healer who treats the ailments of the heart and must therefore be able to see clearly with the Eye of the Heart precisely what the disciple's needs are at each stage of the journey and to intervene, even at a distance, when necessary. These qualifications were possessed fully by Imām al-Ḥaddād. "We have a mirror," he said, "with which we look at hearts." And Sayyid Aḥmad ibn Zayn al-Ḥabashī said, "I saw Sayyidī ᶜAbdallāh in a dream vision and he said to me 'God has bestowed upon us everything that is needed to take the people to Him, but they showed no eagerness.'" Sayyid Aḥmad then added that he related the dream to the Imām who confirmed its reality saying, "It is so!"

The function of the master is to take the people to God, never allowing them to rest short of the very limit of their natural aptitudes. This may take seconds if the seeker comes already qualified, and there are indeed rare instances when the traveler receives his Opening on his first meeting with the *shaykh*; or it may take long years of effort and patience to reach the same point. The Imām is reported to have said, "The great saints are like the sun and the wick ready to catch fire. When a seeker comes to them who is qualified, they set him alight instantaneously, when not, they train him until he qualifies. Thereafter their states [i.e., the seekers] vary. Some are like good wicks which take fire from the first time and thus become transformed, but upon whom no outward sign appears during their lifetime, just as a lamp is not seen in the presence of the sun. Others catch fire after repeated attempts, and others still not at all, like the ailment which no medicine can alter. Then, having been set alight, some remain firmly so, others are extinguished immediately, and others after a while, according to how well suited they had been for it." This 'setting alight' is the initial and most essential spiritual transmission, the first effective step on the path, frequently likened to the sowing of seeds or the pollination of palm trees. During the Imām's visit to the town of Shibām, a man came to him with his young son and asked him to look after him and 'pollinate' him. The Imām passed his hand over the boy's head. Many years later, now grown, he went to visit the Imām in Tarim in the company of a number of his townsmen. As each of them greeted the Imām he asked them, as was his custom, how they were and to which family each belonged. When it was the young man's turn to take the Imām's hand, to his surprise, instead of asking him the usual questions he said, "You are the pollinated one, are you not?"

To accomplish the required task, each spiritual master uses a method (*ṭarīqa*), transmitted to him from his own chain of spiritual masters and capable of being modified, within certain limits, by gnostic *shaykhs* to suit the changing conditions of the times. The sober and strictly orthodox ᶜAlawī method was the heritage of Imām al-Ḥaddād. The Imām described it as, "The most straightforward and upright…its soundness is born witness to by the Book, the *Sunna*, and history of our virtuous predecessors. They received it from their forefathers, up to the Prophet, may God's blessings and peace be upon him." He also said, "Our school is the Book, the *Sunna,* and the way of the virtuous predecessors in all but a few rare things in which we conform to the pattern of theses times." The Imām explained that different methods are outwardly divergent but one in their essence in these terms: "The paths of Sufism, though numerous, are but one path, which is to wage war against the ego and resist it in everything it incites; and this is a difficult matter." He further stated, "Our method is that of al-Ḥasan al-Baṣrī," the latter having been the chief disciple of Imām ᶜAlī and thus the spiritual ancestor of almost all existing Sufi chains.

The particular form taken by the ᶜAlawī method in the days of Imām al-Ḥaddād, he termed the 'Method of the Companions of the Right Hand' (*ṭarīqat ahl'al-yamīn*), thus distinguishing it from that used in earlier generations which he termed the 'Method of the Drawn Near' (*ṭarīqat al-muqarrabīn*). This first method begins by imposing on its adherents the practice of the general or common pattern with sincerity and excellence. According to Imām al-

Ḥaddād, the general way is for the disciple to occupy the whole of his time with acts of worship and remembrance, guard himself from transgressions, and concentrate on the hereafter. When he masters these, he is then promoted to a more intense form of traveling—the 'special method,' which is to "divest oneself outwardly and inwardly from all that is not God." The implication is that every single action must conform to what is pleasing to God, be intended purely for His sake, in total reliance upon Him, and that one's whole inner life be fixed on the Absolute, allowing for no contingent distractions. One has then to "discard reprehensible attributes, in detail, and acquire praiseworthy ones, in detail." This means that one must identify each individual imperfection in his own character, strive to erase it, and replace it with the corresponding virtue. "We train some men from among our children for years to acquire a single virtue," said the Imām. Yet, having said this, he still maintained that this method was not that of the elite. "Never think that we are on the path of the elect," said he. "For rare are those who request it with sincerity. We are on the general path, the path of the Companions of the Right Hand." And he said, "Retreats and asceticism are inappropriate in this age that lacks their specific conditions, such as licit provision and other things. Those who base their affair on maintaining their obligatory acts of worship, avoiding prohibited things, performing what supererogatory acts they can, enjoining good and forbidding evil, assisting the weak, helping the needy or taking charge of his expenses, and other similar things, and firmly keep to this, may yet obtain that which [earlier people] had obtained through their asceticism and retreats." However, he also said, "In these times, perform the good works that are not too strenuous for you and in which you are able to persevere. For a little that is constant is better than much that is interrupted. Give thanks for the little granted you and God will give you more. Do not look at the states of such people as Bishr, al-Fudayl, and their peers. For even the Companions, may God be pleased with them, did not do as much as they, though they had the light of Prophethood. Someone once said when asked about this, 'The Companions had more faith and the Followers more works.' And where is your time compared with theirs? You are now in the twelfth century!" That he had something more to offer but found very few people to accept it was one of the recurrent themes in the Imām's conversations. He often stated that if he had found those who would shoulder adequately the responsibility for summoning the masses to the straight path of the common people, he would have devoted himself to the path of the elect.

"The science of Sufism has been folded up," the Imām once said, "but we have been permitted to unfold it." And when one of his close disciples asked him, "When someone comes to you who knows nothing of the path of the predecessors or of that of the Companions of the Right Hand, what should he do?" he replied, "He should do as we are doing; he should observe and mimic our actions, which is as you see the correct performance of the ritual prayers, recitation of the Qur'ān, regular invocations, seeking beneficial knowledge, and persevering in all this. Have you ever heard of any of the scholars of the two Sanctuaries or elsewhere doing this and being criticized for it, or heard anyone criticizing this method?" "No!" answered the disciple. "This is the path of the Companions of the Right Hand," continued the Imām, "and it is the appropriate one. The people of this time should be placed on the common path, for the path of the elect is impracticable. Otherwise how many think themselves to be like Shaykh ᶜAbdal-Qadīr, when they are not worth a thorn in his foot?"

There are priorities for the seeker on the path. He must first "establish soundly the principle of *tawḥīd*, then discharge his obligations and avoid all prohibitions, and thirdly perform the *sunnas* as stated in the Book and *Sunna* without exceeding them. When these things bear their fruits much good will come to him." And in a letter to Sayyid ᶜAlawī ibn Shaykh al-Jufrī, then in India, he writes, "As for taking from the *shaykh* you mention, there is no harm in this provided that his path does not differ from that which is ours and which our companions receive both by example and by word of mouth. For the paths to God are numerous, some are alike and some differ in their outward forms, not in their essence. The traveler in his beginnings travels according to the outward form, however, until he goes beyond it and reaches the essential realities, and that only after many experiences. As for our method, it needs on the whole no explanation, for it is the Book and *Sunna* and following our virtuous predecessors and nothing more. This summary description comprises many lengthy details. Had we found among the people of this time those whose quest, aspiration, resolution, and fervor were as sincere as they should have been, we would have expounded it to them in detail, explaining what of it is of specific and what of general import, what is suitable for some and what for others. The method of the people of Hindustan is similar and akin to ours. They are mostly reserved, conforming to the Book and *Sunna*, and circumspect in religious matters. But there are *ṭarīqas* in some regions of the Deccan land and other regions in Eastern India, which are wholly or mostly devilish, abhorrent, and leading to the wrath of God and that of

His Messenger. We ask God to grant us and you safety from temptations."

The question that arises in the minds of many seekers, once they have grasped the distinction between the two methods, is whether they will differ in their results. That is, whether the easier method could possibly result in a degree of purification sufficient to lead to gnosis. The Imām answered this by saying, "It is an easy path that leads the person who perseveres in it to catch up with the people of the other path, for he may yet attain to Openings on this path, which lead him to catch up with those on the other. Of the path of the predecessors it contains a little of almost everything. It is an easy path with no forty days retreat, no exertion, and no danger. As for the path of the predecessors, it is wearisome for there are forty days retreats, and it has dangers...." Some of these dangers shall be discussed later in this chapter.

Guidance in the way of teaching and providing advice appropriate to most situations may be performed by anyone with enough knowledge and experience of the method. Inward spiritual assistance, however, is only possible when a firm inward bond (*rābiṭa*) has been established between the *shaykh* and the disciple. This is why the Imām wrote in answer to a question that there are three kinds of *shaykhs*: the *shaykh* of teaching provides the formal knowledge of *Sharīᶜa*, the *shaykh* of discipline guides the seeker in his struggle against his ego but does not provide the inward support which can only be provided by the *shaykh* of the Opening. This latter *shaykh* is the only one worthy of being called a spiritual master.

Spiritual transmission is on its own plane quite similar to electricity on the material plane. Just as the flow of electricity depends on the conduction of the cable, the thicker it is, the less the resistance and the greater the flow; so it is with spiritual transmission, the more powerful the bond, the less the resistance, and the greater the flow. "The pillar of this path," said the Imām, "is the strength of the bond. When strong, no accidents can damage it." The onus for the preservation and strengthening of this bond falls on the disciple, for the *shaykh* gives only to those who ask. Far from being a mere verbal exercise, asking in this context indicates a sincere movement of the heart toward the *shaykh* signifying that it is open and ready to receive the spiritual flow that comes. This can happen once the disciple commits himself entirely to the *shaykh*, in the certainty that he will respond to his heart's specific needs. Imām al-Ḥaddād once likened it to a rope stretching from the *shaykh* to the disciple. "When you are holding a rope in your hand, and then let go of it, you are the one to blame, not the rope. The elect and the virtuous care for you as much as you care for them. A man once said to Abul-ᶜAbbās al-Mursī, 'Keep me in mind,' to which he replied, 'You keep me in mind.'" Then the Imām added the provision that "only those benefit whose hearts are strong in belief and illumined, whereas those whose belief is weak and hearts dark do not benefit." And he also said, "The way of the Bā-ᶜAlawī *sayyids* consists of holding sound doctrinal belief, attachment to the *shaykh*, [spiritual] solicitude from the *shaykh*, and refinement by means of the "secret." It is the way of the predecessors such as al-Ḥasan al-Baṣrī and others." The 'secret' by means of which the *shaykh* refines the disciple is not to be confused with the highest level in the hierarchy, beginning from below and moving upward with the body, the soul or *nafs*, the spirit or *rūḥ*, and finally the secret or *sirr*. Rather it is the special attribute invested in the master, which enables him to perform his function. It is through the influence of this *sirr* that the disciple is promoted from one station to another. This was expressed by Shaykh Abū Bakr ibn Sālim thus: "When they look at him, they cause him to reach the highest degree with God, that which cannot be expressed [verbally]." It is also through the 'secret' that the *shaykh* recognizes those whom God wishes to entrust to him, distinguishing them from those belonging to others masters, and attracting them to him. Said the Imām, "Our custom is that, when we want someone, we pull him to us, even if he is in the most remote place; and those we do not want we banish, even though they may remain [in appearance] near to us."

It is the saint's nature to love whatever God loves and this naturally involves the seekers of God. Being the *khalīfa* and having donned the Divine Attributes to replace his human imperfections, he then feels and behaves towards the seekers in exactly the manner that God wishes him to. The Imām used to say, "We love and look after everyone whom we see eager to tread the path to God the Exalted." And, "I rejoice for the seeker who is true with himself, for he thus assists me with the *baraka* of his sincerity to take him along the path." For the *shaykh's* love and solicitude will evidently differ in intensity according to the disciple's sincerity, conformity, and yearning. He once quoted the well known *ḥadith qudsī*, applying it to the relationship between himself and his disciple: "Those who draw nearer to us a handspan, we draw nearer to them the length of an arm, and those who draw nearer to us the length of an arm we draw nearer to them two arms' lengths."[29] He was more explicit on another occasion and spelled out what the disciples, whom he generously called companions, had to do to deserve his full solicitude, "The companion in our view is he who keeps God's company with thorough courtesy, which entails heeding His injunctions, avoiding His prohibitions, surrendering to His might, being very thankful to Him, keeping the heart free from all other than Him, and remaining ever needy for His favors and goodness." Lesser degrees of sincerity and rectitude still gain immensely from their attachment to the *shaykh*, however. Once when one of his companions complained to him about some of his worries he was told, "We are with you, and those we are with have nothing to fear." The man said, "Even though we are neglectful and defective?" to which the answer was, "Aloofness would be unbecoming on our part after reconciliation." He was also heard going even further in saying, "Those whom we have known we never allow to perish, nor do we ever abandon them, even if they abandon us and sever the cord with their own hands."

The Imām's biographer, Sayyid Muḥammad ibn Sumayṭ, recounts the story of a man who, although professing to be extremely attached to the *shaykh*, was nevertheless said to be far from upright in his behavior. The *shaykh* frequently upbraided him, but to no avail. One day he warned him, "Wring yourself out by repenting before they wring you with chastisement." The warning went unheeded and shortly afterward the man was arrested, put in chains, imprisoned, and heavily fined. He remained in prison for a long while, then the Imām interceded on his behalf and he was released. When they met he asked him how he was, to which the man retorted, "You tell me how you are with me!" "We are with you," he answered him, "each time you stumble we shall take you by the hand." Not long after this the man died and was seen by another in a dream vision who inquired, "How has God dealt with you?" He replied, "There were abasements and elevations, then the letter of Sayyidī ᶜAbdallāh ibn ᶜAlawī al-Ḥaddād arrived and dispersed all these matters and I was released from the fear of them." The fact that the Imām was able to help this man after his death by intervening in another world is a reminder that remoteness in physical space will form even less of an obstacle to the *shaykh's* solicitude for his disciples in this world. The Imām is on record as saying, "Those who are attached to us and upon whom we have cast our gaze we never let go, even when they are far away from us... they should follow the example of the one they have become attached to, and the rest we shall carry on their behalf." It has even been said that the disciple who is remote in space is more likely to benefit from his master. When the Imām was asked, "Which is better and more agreeable to you, a man who is remote in space but strongly attached to the *shaykh* or another who is always with him but whose attachment is weaker?" He replied, "The one more strongly attached is better than the other, even though the latter may be present, for a great deal of profit lies in attachment that can be obtained in no other way, even though presence offers other advantages." He was again asked, "Does not that which the one who is here obtains, of seeing, meeting, praying with you and learning from you, equal the attachment of the absentee?" He replied with an emphatic "No!" and explained it by saying that remoteness preserves the election aspect of the *shaykh* whereas intimate contact emphasizes the human side to the detriment of the hidden spiritual side. Respect and reverence might thus suffer, with a corresponding decrease in attachment and emulation.

Despite their insistence on the bond, the ᶜAlawīs are very careful not to stand between the seeker and the Prophet, may blessings and peace be upon him. When someone told the Imām that the spiritual assistance (*madad*) they receive was from him, he did not deny it, but replied, "Spiritual assistance is but from the Prophet, may God's blessings and peace be upon him, and our assistance comes from him." This explains such remarks as the following, which might at first sight seem to contradict what was said earlier about the importance of the bond between the master and the disciples, "Men of God like the people to be little attached to them, but rather to concentrate on God and His Messenger."

Another prominent ᶜAlawī attribute is extreme circumspection. The Imām was always extremely reserved concerning the spiritual status of his disciples for fear of exposing them to the perils of conceit, self-admiration, and ostentation. He very seldom praised any of them to their faces, for when a man praised another in the presence of the Prophet, may God's blessings and peace be upon him, he told him, "You have cut your brother's throat; had he heard it he would never have succeeded."[30] Some of his companions he spoke of after their deaths, revealing their merits. Others he praised but only after they had achieved enough mastery to be safe from the dangers involved, and even then, with no more than one or two words. This pattern, as with most everything else in the Imām's behavior, remains the ᶜAlawī pattern to this day. Despite total envelopment of their disciples in their spirituality and inward elevation from one rank to the next, ᶜAlawī masters do not allow signs of this to appear outwardly. Many of their disciples receive their Openings only in the safety of the *barzakh*. The Imām once said, 'We hide the special attributes of our companions within their human aspects." And Imām Aḥmad ibn Zayn commented on this statement by saying, "They may outwardly exhibit certain things that may veil from the onlooker, and sometimes even from themselves, whatever special distinctions and *madad* they possess. They hardly ever perceive themselves as possessing a spiritual state, nor do they ever claim a station as their own, and in most situations they feel that they lack sincerity with God." And Imām al-Ḥaddād was heard stating, "Our companions do not see their states until in the hereafter." This does not prevent the *shaykh* from using his spiritual power to direct upon their hearts a constant flow of light which gradually removes the 'rust' and affects their souls in such a way as to give them a distinctive character immediately recognizable by those possessed of the Opening. "Our companions are marked," said the Imām, "they can thus be recognized by those whose vision is clear." And the gnostic *sayyid* Aḥmad al-Hunduwān said in effect, "I recognize the companions of Sayyidī ᶜAbdallāh and am able to distinguish them from other people; they bear the marks of their prostration on their faces!" One of his closest disciples who believed himself to be a failure was ᶜAbdal-Raḥmān ibn ᶜAbdal-'Aẓīm Bā-Sharāḥīl. Once during the course of a teaching session he sat there, criticizing himself for having kept the Imām's company for so long without changing for better. The Imām read his thoughts but said nothing until the session ended. Only when he took his hand for permission to leave did he tell him, "You are too weak for the *ḥāl*, but there is *baraka* in you."

The *madad* of the Imām carried his disciples on their ascent despite the weakness in their souls. He protected them from their own imperfections, humored them, and maintained his solicitude for them despite their sometimes straying off the path, which led to a setback corresponding in magnitude to their deviation. "Some of our companions may suffer a halt," he said, "but they mostly end up returning to the straight path." And he also said, "Those whom we come to know we abandon neither to shame nor to the flame." He strove to correct even relatively minor misdemeanors. One of his disciples once sat with some other people in the Imām's house in Tarīm while the latter was in his other house at al-Ḥāwī. There were jesters in the group whose words were frivolous and at times crude. The next morning the Imām sent for his disciple and, hitting him repeatedly with something he had in his hand, repeated to him everything that had been said the night before, reproaching him for having sat with them.

He also always urged them to expend more effort in purifying their hearts in order to be able to receive more *madad*. For the masters are ever keen to give as much as possible to their disciples, the limitation lying in the latters' receptivity. When the son of one of his late companions once came to him with a request that he secretly whispered in his ear, the Imām answered, "Purify your soil and prepare it, then when you have done so come to us, for we possess all the seeds." And when another man, overcome by some secret longing, wept in his presence, he was told, "Weeping is for women, men do not weep; it is their hearts that do. Spiritual states are not to be acquired by weeping, but by striving." Then he turned to the others saying, "One of two things is necessary for saints; some of them dig for the treasure, while others have their spirits attached to the Throne. One of these two is necessary. The spiritual states of some saints are shouldered at their death by forty men, others divide them between sixty men." Then addressing the man again he said, "Carry on as you are and your apportioned share will come to you."

Solicitude from the *shaykh* and efforts from the disciple must eventually bear their fruits of gnosis. However, it seems that it is only after physical separation from the *shaykh* that most disciples begin to show the expected results. Mention has already been made of how the disciple who dies before his *shaykh* finds his Opening awaiting him in the security of the *barzakh*. The two other modes of separation are the disciple's return to his homeland and the *shaykh's* death. The first was brought out in a conversation between the Imām and one of the numerous foreign disciples who came to Tarīm; for he complained to the *shaykh* that he perceived in himself no sign of his having benefited from his company. The *shaykh* reassured him that he had indeed 'taken root and produced fruits," but that for fear of the dangers of self-admiration and pride his current condition was better for him. Then he added that it was the rule for the signs of this not to appear on a man as long as he was in the presence of his teacher. As for the second mode, which is when the *shaykh* dies before the disciple, there is then the added factor of the *shaykh's* spiritual state being shared among his disciples. The Imām writes in his treatise on the *Good Manners of the Spiritual Disciple*, "When you see the disciple full of reverence and respect for his *shaykh*, outwardly and inwardly collected in his faith in him and obedience to him, know that he will inevitably inherit all or some of his secret should he survive him." Many years later he was to say, "Some of our companions will be seen to increase following our departure from this world; this is because they had sincerity when they kept our company."

The Imām was also extremely reticent when it came to responding to his disciples' curiosity concerning the Unseen. He made his reasons abundantly clear on many occasions but also indicated what they had to do to receive such knowledge. On two occasions when written questions were submitted to him concerning the Pole, he answered with no more than quoting what other men of God had said, adding very little in the way of comment. He then writes, "The gist of all this is that looking into the realities and subtleties of the sciences of the People of the Path should be allowed only to those who are proficient in the outward sciences, who have mastered them, then disciplined their souls and refined them to perfection, then been taken by a Divine pull from Him to annihilate the remainder of their human nature, which thing cannot be achieved by effort." Elsewhere , he specified the effort required, "Whosoever desires this *kashf* (unveiling of some of the unseen) should discipline his soul, reduce its density with the kind of arduous effort that annihilates the soul's frivolity and conquers its passions, and he should embellish it with concentration on God the Exalted, with courtesy, submissiveness, humility, powerlessness, and poverty in the realization of slavehood (*ᶜubūdiyya*) and the fulfilling of the rights of Lordship (*rubūbiyya*). Whenever a servant masters these two basic things, effective discipline and perfect presence, the veil over his heart is rent and he beholds the Unseen of his Lord, and he sees the saints, in their ranks and holy functions, as pure spirits. He will then no longer need any descriptions and will rise from the troughs of learning from others to the peak of contemplation." And in the course of his commentary on a gnostic poem by the younger ᶜAydarūs, he quotes a few verses from ibn al-Fāriḍ on extinction and subsistence, explains these states briefly, then adds that "a full exposition of this matter would be very lengthy, and moreover, would involve subtle concepts and hidden mysteries that are not to be entrusted to the pages of a book, lest they be read by the unqualified, who might then claim these states as their own and thus stray from the Straight Path." This danger is very real and we do indeed see many people these days who assiduously read Ibn al-ᶜArabī and Jīlī and think that this is the reality of Sufism, mistaking theoretical knowledge for realization. The Imām also writes, "...otherwise, those who continuously look into the subtleties of these sciences, while not in the state of perfection that we have just described, will only emerge from one problem to fall into the next. They may become perplexed and unable to decide what to do, and they may be subject to other things of a more difficult nature."

Numerous would-be Sufis are preoccupied with Ibn al-ᶜArabī and Ibn al-Fāriḍ, and the Imām had thus many occasions to comment on their works. When he received a letter from one of his more knowledgeable disciples inquiring about certain problematic statements in Shaykh Ibn al-ᶜArabī's writings, he wrote back saying, "Know that there are many problematic matters in the *shaykh's* books, particularly in the "*Futūḥāt*"[31] and the "*Fuṣūṣ*".[32] These may have been either introduced into the *shaykh's* writings by others or produced by him when overpowered by a spiritual state and under the overwhelming influence of an essential reality... or the *shaykh* may have expressed it in such a manner as to conceal secrets and meanings too subtle to be put into words. The *shaykh* is one of those who has a firmly established position in the sciences, gnoses, *taqwā*, and detachment from the world. It is thus improper for any Godfearing person, aware of these things about the *shaykh*, to accuse him of straying from the truth...." He was also heard saying, "Ibn ᶜArabī speaks of essential realities while at the same time maintaining utmost respect for the law and being knowledgable in all sciences." And, comparing him with Ibn al-Fāriḍ, he said, "His beliefs and behavior are of the utmost rectitude, but not his words; yet his words are nearer to safety than those of Ibn-al-Fāriḍ, since he seldom mentions an essential reality without backing it up with ten statements of impeccable legality." And he warned that "The soul is attracted to his words and repelled by the words which carry its remedy and may lead to its cure, which are those of Imām al-Ghazālī; for it is in the nature of the soul to flee that which is of benefit to it and incline toward that which is of harm."

As concerns Ibn al-Fāriḍ, the Imām was known to have enjoyed his poetry since his early teens and he later had the whole *Dīwān* recited before him during the Tuesday afternoon session, saying, "These are the words of a heart that is alive in a body that is dead." Yet he always bid the reciter to pass over the *Tā'iyya*,[33] it being too full of hidden realities and thus too apt to be misunderstood. Shaykh ibn al-Fāriḍ died at the age of fifty five, for "the people of spiritual states seldom live very long, for they are taken by their states. Such was Shaykh Abū Bakr al-Sakrān and his son Shaykh ᶜAbdallāh [al-ᶜAydarūs], who lived about fifty years, and so it has been with others." He also said that both Ibn al-Fāriḍ and Ibn ᶜArabī possessed the same art, however, "Ibn ᶜArabī is mostly more sober and Ibn al-Fāriḍ mostly more absorbed."

To avoid the dangers in gnostic poetry, the Imām taught that "when a created being speaks of the attributes of created beings, the appropriate thing is to ascribe them to a created being." Thus, "love poetry should be understood as the soul addressing the spirit, not as referring to Divine matters, since these are difficult to comprehend and mysterious. Only the greatest *ṣiddīqūn* understand them." And, "Attribute what you hear to the spirit or to the Kaᶜba, for there is no danger in that, but do not pass beyond that to Prophethood or the angels or the Divinity, for the limit of the knowledge of the angels is the Lote Tree of the Limit." The Imām's opinion was that it was very much discouraged to write love poetry addressed to the Muḥammadan

Mausoleum of the Sultan of Lovers, Shaykh ᶜUmar ibn al-Fāriḍ at the foot of the Muqaṭṭam Hills in Cairo.

Grave of Shaykh ᶜUmar ibn al-Fāriḍ within.

Spirit, as well as being discourteous and dangerous. He also said, however, "Much of their love poetry refers to the Muḥammadan Spirit and the most sublime stations, for he, may peace be on him, is a created being, and danger regarding a created being is still acceptable, even though his rank may be immense, may peace be on him, and they do maintain their reverence and respect for him to the utmost."

As for his own poetry, whatever was felt by him to be potentially dangerous and had been composed under the influence of spiritual states, he would allow no one to see, not even after his death. His *Dīwān* was compiled during his lifetime and since no other poetry was discovered after his death, it is to be assumed that he had destroyed it himself for fear of it being found by the unqualified and misunderstood. Someone had once told him that he read such books as we have just been mentioning and whatever he understood he took and whatever he did not he left well alone, to which the Imām's answer was that he was not concerned with what was not understood but with what was believed to have been understood but had in fact been misunderstood.

There are other dangers on the path, even for those who, having fulfilled some of the conditions that we have mentioned above, are in the early stages of realization. They may overestimate their state and believe that they have reached stations that are in reality still a long way off. They may lose control under the influence of too powerful a state and produce utterances that are considered by others, with some justification, as sheer blasphemy. Or they may abandon their legally binding acts of worship under the pretext that they have 'arrived' and no longer need them. Other effects of powerful states on unprepared travelers turn them into ecstatics, *majdhūbs* and in more extreme cases they may even perish. As Imām al-Ḥaddād once said of a certain *sayyid*, "He has plunged into the ocean of love headlong, and it has killed him; he has no more than six months to live. As for us, we have prepared ships for it and it has not affected thus." It should be clear by now why every traveler needs a powerful *shaykh* to protect him against such hazards, until he himself reaches the station where he becomes immune from them. This occurs only when he enters the presence of the Prophet, may God's blessings and peace be upon him, and becomes firmly established therein, at which stage he is said to be 'guarded' (*maḥfūẓ*) and to have himself become a master.

Other problems arise as a consequence of unveiling. The first is that if there remains some weakness in the traveler and his attaining to unveiling results in self-admiration, then he is inevitably dispossessed and reverts to the status of a commoner. The second problem might be intensely unpleasant. The Imām once said, "As for the matter of unveilings, it is not appropriate in this time. When they occur to someone, they cause him to regret this and wish that they had not come to pass. Suppose that it is revealed to you that a certain man hates and insults you, what would you do to him? Would you go and beat him? No, such things are better kept hidden. A certain man of God who had disciplined himself thoroughly once saw a group of people approaching a well. He saw some of them in the form of dogs, others as pigs, and so on, for God revealed them to him in their subtle forms and he prayed that God veil him once again from them." What this man had seen was the forms of those people in the World of Similitudes (*ᶜālam al-mithāl*), where things appear, as in dreams, in the form corresponding to their most dominant attribute. This is the lowest degree of unveiling and may be quite unsettling for the traveler who passes through it. By definition, travelers should be disinterested in the affairs of created beings and wary of distractions. They are therefore ever imploring their Lord to veil these sights from them. Furthermore, revealing what they see is rarely permitted and those who do so may suffer costly setbacks. "Inward knowledge is secret," said the Imām, "and it is forbidden to divulge it. Suppose a man came to consult you about a voyage that he intends to take, and you know that he is to die in a month, or that something is to happen to him, would you inform him of it and advise him to stay? No! Neither did the Prophet do it, nor the Companions, yet the truth had been unveiled before them, for they were more worthy of unveiling than anyone else."

There are lesser problems that are still worth mentioning since they concern the relationship between the disciple and his *shaykh* and consequently the degree to which he benefits from him. Treatises on Sufism are unanimous in stating that the disciple should be as accepting of the authority of the *shaykh* as the "corpse in the hands of the washer of the dead." The principle here is that the more passive he is with what is higher than him, the more active he becomes with what is lower. Thus, the more passive and receptive he is to the influence of the higher worlds, the more active and effective he becomes in his influence upon the lower worlds, which are the ego inwardly and the social and material environment outwardly. As Imām al-Ḥaddād made it clear, however, this applies unconditionally only to the *shaykh* of *taḥkīm* and to the path of the elect. The general path, on the other hand, permits much lesser degrees of passivity, since it involves the generality of believers at its first level and then becomes gradually more demanding until it merges imperceptibly with the threshold of the path of the elect. This is why the Imām, having defined the legal boundaries of each matter, did nothing to impose his views on the people around him. He counselled his close disciples not to oppose the wishes of those who came to them for advice in saying, "When their heart is set on something and they have decided to do it, you should not advise them to leave it, for if you do they will disobey you, or if they comply it will be reluctantly and with some effort." And he said, "When someone consults us about something and we find in him an inclination for that matter, we advise him to go through with it, unless it be unlawful. When we perceive no inclination in him, then we advise him with what we see fit." Nevertheless, he encouraged this particular kind of compliance in his disciples, to accelerate their traveling and avoid pitfalls. "The seeker should not say, 'Command me to do this, or give me that.' Rather let him be as a dead body in the hands of the washer. If they choose something for him without his asking, let him obey. Otherwise, let him stop, for he knows not what is good for him and they know better; for people differ. For some, only serving the *shaykh* is good, for others only serving the disciples is good, and for others still neither is good; according to the difference in their instincts and natures." The affectation of passivity, however, he disliked intensely. When one of his guests once asked permission to leave, using a choice of words to imply that the matter was entirely in the *shaykh's* hands, he became angry and said, "Do not do this lest I order you to stay for a month or two; how discomfited will you be then?" He then gave them as an example his own behavior towards his *shaykh*, Sayyid ᶜUmar al-ᶜAṭṭās. When the *shaykh* had bid him stay as he had asked permission to leave, he had said, "If you wish me to stay I shall, but if it is for fear of the rain, then God willing, we shall not suffer from it." His guidelines on the appropriate courtesy to be observed by the disciple with his *shaykh* form one of the last chapters of *Good Manners of the Spiritual Disciple* and are amply sufficient, though concise.

There is abundant evidence in the Imām's correspondence of the extent to which his spiritual influence had radiated during his lifetime. He had disciples in Morocco, Egypt, Syria, the Hijāz, the Persian gulf area, Turkey, and India. Shaykh Aḥmad ᶜAbdal-Karīm al-Shajjār, who collected the sayings of the Imām in two large volumes, mentions that there were always in Tarīm a number of foreigners who had come to the Imām as disciples, many of whom remained there for years. Shaykh Aḥmad himself was one of them, better known in Tarīm as al-Ḥasāwī. He lived near the Imām for seventeen years, used to accompany him wherever he went, carrying his prayer rug and sandals. He only returned to his country in the eastern part of the Arabian peninsula after his master's death.

The most prominent disciple of the Imām was undoubtedly Sayyid Aḥmad ibn Zayn al-Ḥabashī, a man of encyclopaedic learning and a major gnostic *shaykh* in his own right. The Imām's sons were also saints and scholars. Many years after his death his son al-Ḥasan was said to have become the Pole of his time. Other disciples who were to become great Imāms were Sayyid ᶜAbdal-Raḥmān Bilfaqīh and Sayyid ᶜUmar ibn ᶜAbdal-Raḥmān al-Bār, who was one of the forty ᶜUmars that Sayyid ᶜUmar al-ᶜAṭṭās had predicted were to reach to God at the hands of Imām al-Ḥaddād. This prediction caused Imām al-Ḥaddād to reassure his family, once when he fell severely ill, that he had been promised to take forty men by the name of ᶜUmar to God and that the number had not been completed yet; he was therefore not to die of that illness. Another ᶜUmar was his younger brother ᶜUmar ibn ᶜAlawī al-Ḥaddād whose descendants were to become the second great branch of al-Ḥaddād's family of saints and gnostics.

Chapter 9
THE SCHOLAR

Different kinds of Islamic sciences—breadth of the Imām's knowledge—jurisprudence, which school?—teaching activities—the Pole of Guidance—meticulous following of the sunna—definition of personal teaching role—the Imām's books.

Islamic knowledge includes several major sciences, each branching into numerous sub-sciences. Consequently, according to his inclination or area of expertise, a scholar (*ᶜālim*) may be better known as a Qur'ānic exegete (*mufassir*), traditionist (*muḥaddith*), or jurisprudent (*faqīh*). Prior to this, however he must have become adequately proficient in the entire range of religious sciences, as well as in the various sciences necessary for the mastery of Arabic as the language of Revelation. The foremost authorities in each of these sciences were accorded the title of Imām, the literal meaning of which is leader. The same title was given to others who were exceptional scholars who had acquired an all-embracing grasp of all these sciences, in addition to other secondary ones such as history, astronomy, and so on.[34] Such Imāms had a profound and widespread influence in their times, and many of them were recognized as the promised "renewers" of religion. Imām al-Ḥaddād belonged undoubtedly to this category. The evidence for this is to be found in his books, letters, poems and collected sayings, as well as in the testimonies of his teachers, contemporaries, and eminent students. One of his teachers, Imām ᶜUmar al-ᶜAṭṭās said of him, "Sayyid ᶜAbdallāh al-Ḥaddād is a nation unto himself." It could not have been said more succinctly and comprehensively. In the course of his *ḥajj* journey, as we shall see, every scholar that he met acknowledged his supremacy and requested his *ijāza*, or authorization. The contemporary grand-mufti of Syria was heard to say in the sacred precinct in Makka, "There is no man on earth today more learned than Sayyid ᶜAbdallah al-Ḥaddād. His book, *al-Naṣā'iḥ* should be read by everyone."

The Imām's companions and disciples noted how no book was ever mentioned in his presence without his being familiar with it. The Imām himself once said, "We do not think that there is a book in the whole of Hadramawt that we have not either read, seen, heard parts of, or heard about." Bearing in mind that Hadramawt was a land of learning and erudition, and that the Imām invariably understated his talents, such a statement is highly meaningful. Equally free from pride or boasting is the following striking statement: "Two favors were bestowed upon us by God the Exalted for which we shall never be able to thank Him adequately. The first is that God, Transcendent be He, has granted us knowledge so extensive that we need the knowledge of no one else on earth, and our soul yearns to meet no one save ᶜAlī ibn ᶜAbdallāh al-ᶜAydarūs.[35] The second favor is that God gave us such a complete intellect that we are in need of no other intellect."

Scholars are generally followers (*muqallid*) of one of the four schools of jurisprudence, and very rarely do they reach independent status (*mujtahid*). The early days came to an end by the third century when there were numerous independent scholars, and the different schools of jurisprudence were founded. Thereafter even those who were said to have reached independent status declared their adherence to one of the four schools, since no more schools were needed and to have attempted to found yet another would have resulted only in confusion and discord. An intermediate class of scholars comprises those who exercise some degree of independent judgment within the boundaries of their own school. Even for these scholars the qualifications were exceedingly stringent. The great Imām al-Shāfiᶜī once said, "None should pass legal judgments relating to God's religion who is not well versed in the Book of God—that of it which is abrogating and that which is abrogated, that which is clear and that which is ambiguous, its interpretation, its revelation whether (Makkan or Madinan), the purpose of [each verse], and the cause of its revelation. He should also be proficient in the *ḥadith* of the Messenger of God, may God's blessings and peace be upon him, the abrogating and the abrogated. He should know about *ḥadith* what he knows about the Qur'ān, and he should be well-versed in Arabic, poetry, and everything else that is necessary to the religious sciences and the Qur'ān. He should be fair-minded and of few words, he should know the differences between the inhabitants of different regions and should possess the gift of understanding. Only then is he to speak and issue legal judgments as to what is lawful and what is not. Otherwise he should not speak of religious knowledge nor issue legal judgments." Followers of a school should know the textual support for every rule of opinion within their school, whereas independent scholars should know the textual evidence behind the position of all four schools as well as scholars such as the *Ẓāhiriyya* and others who do not belong to these and have the ability to weigh them against each other.

Imām al-Ḥaddād was a *mujtahid* despite his strict adherence to the Shāfiᶜī school. On more than one occasion he explained the Shāfiᶜī ruling concerning a particular is-

The Nuwaydira Mosque built by Imām al-Ḥaddād.

Teaching room on the first floor of the house at al-Ḥāwī.

sue, then declared that he had a different opinion but would keep it to himself. Sometimes he would also state that on certain issues he preferred the position of Imām Mālik. He even went so far on some occasions as to declare that, had he not adopted the Shāfiᶜī school because it was that of his ᶜAlawī ancestors he would have adopted that of Imām Mālik. For in his opinion, the way Mālik had depended for the transmission of the Prophetic *sunna* on the pattern of the people of Madina was reliable. He was heard on a few rare occasions declaring that his school was the Book and *sunna*, which is another way of saying that he derived his knowledge directly from Revelation without the intermediary of another Imām.

Imām al-Ḥaddād remained a tireless teacher for over sixty years. He began his first formal teaching circle at al-Hujayra mosque in the year 1071 H., when he was yet twenty-seven years of age. This is how he recalled those days at a much later stage: "We had no wish to teach, but a man from the Bā-Faḍl clan said, 'I wish to take your *baraka* [by reading] whatever will be made easy from "*Riyāḍ al-Sāliḥīn*."'[36] Then Sayyid Ḥasan al-Jufrī came along saying, 'I wish to read whatever will be made easy from "ᶜ*Awārif*."'[37] Then the *faqīh* Bā-Jubayr[38] asked to read *Ḥizb al-Barr*, and from then on reading continued. Following that regular sessions were held daily after ᶜ*Aṣr* and on Thursday and Monday mornings, and continued after the Imām moved to al-Ḥāwī on the outskirts of Tarīm. Other, more informal sessions, were held, where Sufi poems were sung, both his and those of others. The poems of Ibn al-Fāriḍ in particular were often recited during the Tuesday sessions.

Despite the Imām's casual description of how he came to assume the role of teacher and guide, quotations from various sources as well as what we know of these men of

God in general indicate that things were not nearly so simple. The Imām is quoted as having said, "I did not make myself known to the people, nor did I establish myself in this role except after Shaykh al-ᶜAydarūs, ᶜAbdallāh ibn Abū-Bakr came to me and commanded me to do so. I said, *'Above every man of knowledge is one who knows better.'*"[39] This is unequivocal in indicating that he was so averse to publicity that he decided to disobey one of his closest spiritual mentors. He even repeated the same verse again when al-Faqīh al-Muqaddam visited him with the same injunction. Finally, however, the Prophet himself appeared to him, and he was left with no option but to comply. He commented on this on another occasion saying, "I complied and stood in that station, when all that I desired was to roam the wilderness."

During his lifetime, Imām al-Ḥaddād was called the "Pole of Guidance" (*Quṭb al-Irshād*), which indicated that he was the foremost "summoner unto God" of his age. Summoning the people to their Lord is primarily the function of Divine Messengers and Prophets and, by extension, that of the elect among their followers. "Scholars are heirs to the Prophets," says a famous *ḥadith,*[40] it being understood that the scholars referenced are those who not only know but also practice what they know. "To the one who practices what he knows, God will grant the knowledge of that which he does not know," says another *ḥadith.* They also must have traveled a substantial distance along the road of self purification, that of the greater *Jihād*, then they must have received the *ijāza*, or authorization, from their teachers to connect them to the chain of transmission going up to the Prophet, may God's blessings and peace be upon him. Imām al-Ḥaddād practiced what he knew down to the last detail. He was the perfect model for the people to emulate, so thoroughly had the Prophetic *sunna* penetrated his heart and suffused his whole being. He proved to all those who saw or heard about him that it was possible to follow the *sunna* thoroughly in all aspects of one's everyday life. He enjoined others to copy his behavior and those who followed him knew very well that this was their best bid to follow the Prophet, may God's blessings and peace be upon him. The Imām put the seal on his perfect following of the *Sunna* when shortly before his death he let his hair to grow down to his earlobes, declaring that this was the very last *Sunna* remaining for him to perform. This was *da*ᶜ*wa* by example; much more eloquent than words, it gave his spoken and written words the authority and power to penetrate people's hearts.

Books on every topic were read before the Imām, but he advised his diciples to concentrate on the compilation of Imām al-Bukharī for *Ḥadith*, the commentary of al-Baghawī for *tafsīr*, al-Nawawī's *Minhāj* for jurispridence, and al-Ghazālī's *Iḥyā'* for a comprehensive text containing in adequate detail the three dimensions of *Islām*, *Īmān*, and *Iḥsān*, or *sharī*ᶜ*a*, *ṭarīqa*, and *ḥaqīqa*.

He declared that there were enough jurisprudents to relieve him of the obligation to function as one, and that although he may have wished at times to discourse on higher realities, as he was one of the very few men on earth qualified to do so, he lacked the audience capable of assimilating such teachings. Therefore, he deliberately chose to concentrate on the intermediate level, that between outward knowledge and actual inward realization. He taught people to love God and His Messenger and act accordingly. He taught them sincerity and fervor in their acts of worship, trained them in the acquisition of the virtues inwardly and the thorough practice of the Sunna outwardly in their relationship with created beings. This is what he believed that the nation needed above all else and this is what he expounded in his writings.

His first work, dictated in 1069 H. (1659 C.E.), *Risālat al Mudhākara*[41] is a short treatise intended to motivate its readers to rearrange their priorities so as to put God and the life-to-come first. It begins with a definition of *taqwā,* and then proceeds to provide convincing evidence from the Qur'ān, the Prophetic traditions, and the utterances of the acknowledged saints and scholars concerning the worthlessness and transience of this world and the superiority of the next and of things spiritual.

His second treatise, *Ādāb Sulūk al-Murīd,*[42] dictated in 1071 H. (1661 C.E.) is a concise basic manual for the serious would be Sufi.

A letter he sent to Shaykh ᶜAbdal Raḥmān Bā-ᶜAbbād of Shibām in 1072 H. (1662 C.E.), in answer to questions the *shaykh* had asked him during his visit to Shibām, became a self-contained treatise, *Itḥāf al-Sā'il.*[43] The Imām included as its conclusion a penetrating commentary on a poem about spiritual growth and attainment by Imām Abū-Bakr al-ᶜAydarūs of Aden. The said Bā-ᶜAbbād was a scholar from Shibām who on first contact with the Imām experienced an intense dislike for him and criticized his behavior. The Imām later remarked concerning this first contact, "The pattern is familiar, scholars that deny the inner dimensions and special attributes that the Sufis claim for themselves, if it is their destiny to join their ranks, they are driven to it, even against their will." This is precisely what happened, for Bā-ᶜAbbād. Having exhibited jealousy and resentment toward the Imām and disinclination to inward knowledge, he was greatly distressed when he suddenly lost his eyesight. He set out with a guide toward the

The Abdāl Mosque in the vicinity of Shibām.

mosque that the Imām had erected in Shibām and where at that moment he was having a session of *dhikr*. The Imām turned to a small boy sitting near him and told him to go to a certain location to fetch Bā-ᶜAbbād, whom he would find there. Bā-ᶜAbbād entered the mosque led by the boy, and, informing the Imām that one of his ancestors, a well known saint by the name of ᶜAbdallāh ᶜAbbād, had come to him to reproach and upbraid him for his discourtesy toward the Imām, apologized and was forgiven and accepted forthwith. Soon afterwards he recovered his eyesight. He seems not to have indicated whether the vision of his ancestor had been during sleep or in his waking state. The Imām, however, took it to be the latter. He said, "We believed him when he said that Shaykh ᶜAbdallah had come to him, for it is our custom to believe all those who come to us." The result of his attachment to the Imām did not fail to make itself evident on Bā-ᶜAbbād, witness a letter by the Imām where he speaks to him in terms implying in no uncertain manner that he had become himself a Sufi. The relevant passage runs as follows: "From ᶜAbdallāh ibn ᶜAlawī al-Ḥaddād ᶜAlawī to the honorable and venerable *shaykh*, truthful and enlightened, ᶜAbdal-Raḥmān ibn ᶜAbdallāh ᶜAbbād, may he discipline his soul under the trampling feet of asceticism, bring out what it hides by plowing it with the cattle of reflection, then water it with the rain of secrets which causes trees to grow and produce fruits. Thus will the end be fulfilled, the beginning having been mastered. This is the explanation of the meaning of guidance opening up into the meaning of election. Take it then with resolution, knowledge, and insight, emulating the experienced, "*if no torrent smites it then dew*," [2:265] Those who belong to neither category have failed and erred…."

A number of letters addressed to various disciples in Hadramawt, Egypt, and elsewhere, containing spiritual advice trimmed down to the bare essentials and spanning the period from 1071 H (1661 CE) to 1107 H (1696 C.E.), were posthumously collected and entitled *al-Waṣāyā al-Nafiᶜa.*[44]

In 1089 H (1678 C.E.) he completed his longest work, *al-Naṣā'iḥ al-Dīniyya*,[45] a comprehensive in-depth exposition of the doctrine and practise of Islam, including the five pillars, enjoining good and forbidding evil, *Jihād*, social responsibilities, the heart's ailments and their remedies, and the necessary virtues. The Imām begins his discussion of these topics with their outward form, subtly proceeding to an examination of their inner spiritual dimension. The *Naṣā'iḥ* was said to represent the quintessence of al Ghazālī's *Iḥyā'*. The Imām once remarked, "We aimed for the book, *al-Naṣā'iḥ*, to be smooth-flowing, clear, intelligible to the one who reads it and has some understanding, so that it may suffice him or, [if it does not, then it should] make him eager for more detailed works."

Risālat'al-Muᶜāwana,[46] dictated in 1099 H (1688 CE), is a manual of how a Muslim should conduct his daily life in all its details, both religious and worldly. In addition, it offers a few most valuable chapters on certainty and its nine stations, expounded in a clear and practical manner.

Ten years elapsed before the Imām dictated *Sabīl al-Iddikār,*[47] a vivid description of the five stages or lives which man passes through in his voyage to immortality. These are the pre-earthly followed by the earthly lives, life in the *Barzakh* or Intermediary Realm, then the events following the Resurrection and leading up to the final separation of those destined for Paradise from those destined for Hell. Again, this work is quintessential and contains everything that one needs to know in order to steer a correct course through each of these stages, thereby avoiding the various pitfalls on the way and eventually eternal torment in Hell.

In 1114 H (1702 C.E.) came his second longest book, *Al-Daᶜwa al-Tāmma,*[48] a unique work in which he classifies society into eight categories: scholars, Sufis and ascetics, kings and rulers, merchants and craftsmen, the poor and the weak, dependents such as women, children, and servants, common people, and finally, non-Muslims. He describes each category's attributes, rights, duties, and the consequences of the influential members of society straying far from the straight path.

In 1125 H (1713 C.E.) Sayyid Aḥmad ibn Zayn al-Ḥabashī extracted from the Imām's correspondence a large number of answers to questions addressed to the Imām by various people over the years, and compiled them in a single volume entitled, *Al-Nafā'is al-ᶜUlwiyya.*[49] These answers cover a wide range of subjects, from ordinary questions on jurisprudence to complex Sufi matters and a discussion of the Circle of Sainthood and the Pole of the Time. Many of these are considered tremendous gifts by Sufi adherents.

In 1130 H (1718 C.E.) appeared *al-Fuṣūl al ᶜIlmiyya*,[50] a collection of forty chapters of which some had been dictated and circulated among the disciples twenty years earlier. The Imām initially wished to wait until the chapters reached forty, but one of his close disciples asked him for the first twenty and he allowed him and others to copy and use them. The only thread which lends the collection internal consistency is that, again, its contents are most valuable for the serious seeker. In it he will learn about priorities, which sciences to acquire from the large number existing, how to steer a middle course in all his affairs, how to structure his time, choose his companions, and distinguish between good and evil in various situations. He will also learn the definition of many an essential concept to help him keep his thinking clear and goal oriented.

A small collection of aphorisms appeared later and was at the time included with his *Dīwān* and collected correspondence in a single volume. Later on it was added to the compilation of his treatises printed in Cairo in the 1970's.

The Imām's correspondence was collected at his bidding during his lifetime and has since appeared in print in two large volumes in Cairo, in 1979 C.E.

His utterances were collected by Shaykh Aḥmad ᶜAbdal-Karīm al Shajjār, a close disciple who lived in the same house as the Imām during the last sixteen years of the latter's life. They appeared in two volumes in Cairo in 1981, then in a much better production printed in Singapore in 1999 C.E.

The Imām's poems are collected in his *Dīwān* entitled *al-Durr al-Manẓūm.* It is a shoreless ocean. For mature travelers it is a treasury of wisdom, spiritual insights, and indications that render all other books superfluous. In the Imām's own words: "He who has the *Dīwān* needs no other book; we have included in it limitless secrets and wisdom." To emphasise the worth of the *Dīwān* he urged his companions to learn parts of it by heart and declared that when those who did so died, the spirits in the *barzakh* would gather around them to hear them recite the verses they knew because they contained hidden sciences and lights to delight them. When a man asked him whether this was applicable to his poems only or was also a property of the poems of other saints, he replied that this was the exclusive property of his poems, because his was a time so poor in spirituality that only the spirits in the *barzakh* were able to recognize the worth of his words.

The *Dīwān* contains some hundred and fifty poems, not counting those of less than six verses. A good number of these poems were commented upon and explained by various scholars, especially by Sayyid Aḥmad ibn Zayn al-Ḥabashī, who produced his voluminous commentaries during the Imām's lifetime and was instructed by him to concentrate on the more outward aspects of the verses and pass under silence the more profound ones. The longest poem, the *Tā'iyya*, is two hundred and fifty verses long. Permission to write a commentary on it was requested by a scholar of substantial calibre, Sayyid Ismāᶜīl al-Baytī. He was refused on ground that it contained hidden sciences. The Imām probably thought that it was better that these sciences remain veiled, and perhaps that Sayyid al-Baytī would be unable to fathom them all. Indeed, the latter subsequently stated that on reflection he was able to discern no less than fourteen different sciences within this poem. For the same reason, other poems were never exposed to an audience. The last thing that the Imām wanted was to cause confusion in minds accustomed to thinking in material or dogmatic terms. He said that he spoke to no one about these poems for a few days, then, if he still remembered them, he took this as a sign from his Lord that they could be made public. Those poems he was made to forget, either partially or wholly, were those that were considered to have been refused Divine authorization.

The Imām was given the title of "renewer" by many authorities, and this title was readily accepted by everyone. Many things justify this title, including the Imām's status among independent scholars as the most learned man of his time, his total devotion to teaching and *daʿwa*, which made him the "Pole of Guidance," the gift of expression that made his writings suitably brief yet unequivocally clear, profound, and comprehensive, and the widespread diffusion of his works across Islamic lands. His writings are even more suited to our times than to his. They seem to have been written expressly for the present day mentality.

The Messenger of God, may God's blessings and peace be upon him, informed his nation that his time was the spiritual pinnacle from which there could only be subsequently a falling away. He said that each coming year would be worse than the one before it until Muslims, as time approached its end, would reach the stage when most of them would have forgotten the very meaning of *Lā ilāha illa'llāh*. He also said that, to slow down this downward trend, God would raise at the turn of each century those whose function would be to revivify religion. The "renewer" is thus a man of great learning and righteousness, whose task is to reformulate the tenets of religion in the language best suited to the mentality of his time. He emphasizes those aspects that are being neglected, corrects errors and deviations, combats heresies, and clarifies obscure issues. Imām Aḥmad ibn Zayn al-Ḥabashī once said that the renewal of religion involved all three levels of *islām*, *īmān*, and *iḥān*, and that each level was renewed by those who possess mastery over it. He then added that all three functions were united in Imām al-Ḥaddād, and he was therefore the renewer for all three levels. There have been differences of opinion among scholars as to whether the renewal is always to be carried out by a single person. Imām al-Ḥaddād quotes Imām al-Suyūṭī as being of the opinion that there could be more than one renewer for each century.

The supreme renewer is of course the expected Mahdī, whose coming the Prophet announced, may God's blessings and peace be upon him, on countless occasions, giving precise descriptions of the Mahdī's physical appearance, lineage and activities. Imām al-Ḥaddād spoke of him thus: "He shall be raised, this is inevitable; and when the sun shall rise the darkness shall vanish. Some people wish for his coming and pray for it, but solely for worldly reasons. Should he ever assign to some of them that which belongs by right to others, he would not be just but iniquitous. What he will do is divide the contents of the treasury equitably among the people. He will not give some that which belongs by right to others...." He also said, "The Mahdī is a perfect man. His state is to know the Book and *sunna*, as well as the differences of opinion within the nation, to have a complete ability to wage war, destroy the enemies, vanquish his adversaries, whether these be disbelievers or [Muslim] transgressors, establish justice among the Muslims, and support the oppressed against the oppressors." And, "The Mahdī will unite in himself the functions of both Pole and Caliph as had been the case with Sayyidunā ᶜAlī; outward and inward [leadership]. He is the renewer of this religion. The meaning of renewal is to clarify for the people the issues which have caused them to diverge [or deviate] for so long, and he is to pronounce on them according to the truth; he will not invent new things from the Book and *sunna*." One of the Imām's companions said: "He will then need inspiration from the Real to be able to distinguish truth from error." And he replied, "The unveilings of the elect cannot be used in legal matters." He was then asked, "What about the Mahdī?" He replied, "As for the Mahdī, it is an obligation to do as he says, since he has [already] been confirmed by the Law-Giver. His sciences are [Divine] gifts. God shall grant him openings into the meanings of the Book and *sunna*, so that he will pronounce legal judgments in the most perfect manner, the manner that is most pleasing to God and His Messenger. This is the knowledge of the members of the Prophet's household. When Sayyidunā ᶜAlī, may God be pleased with him, was asked, "Has the Messenger of God, may God's blessings and peace be upon him, given you knowledge that was given to no one else?" he said, "No, nothing but some understanding of the Book of God.""

As the renewer, the Imām's positions in matters of doctrine must represent the majority orthodox views, those of *ahl al-sunna wal-jamāᶜa*, and a brief exposé of these is now to follow.

Chapter 10
DOCTRINAL POSITION

Following Imām al-Shāfiᶜī in matters of sacred law and Ashᶜarī in matters of tawḥīd—the creed of Imām al-Ḥaddād—the question of predestination—points of divergence with the Shīᶜa.

As he followed Imām al-Shāfiᶜī in matters of law, despite being an independent authority in his own right, so did Imām al-Ḥaddād adopt the Ashᶜarī position in matters of *Tawḥīd*, despite being a master of gnosis. The Ashᶜarī school represents, together with the Māturīdī school adopted by the Hanafis,[51] the orthodox position common to the great majority of *sunni* Muslims. Imām al-Ḥaddād was once asked, "Is the correct doctrine restricted to that expounded by Ashᶜarī ?" He replied, "His doctrinal exposition is the truth and whatever lies outside it contains both truth and error. He surpassed others because he said, 'I believe in God, in what has come down from Him, in the manner that He wants it,' then he committed himself to Him." These comments, praising Ashᶜarī for restricting himself to textual evidence and not attempting to impose rational interpretations on everything not immediately intelligible, reflect the traditional ᶜAlawī distaste for verbose theology, their strict adherence to the mainstream doctrinal position of the Muslim nation, and reluctance to accord the rational faculty more than its due in discussing such matters. The masters among them have always said, "Strive and you shall see!"[52] This is again clearly to be seen in the Imām's exposition of the doctrine of *Tawḥīd* in his books *al-Naṣā'iḥ al-Dīniyya* and *Itḥāf al-Sā'il.* Because of its power, clarity, and brevity the first of these was later reprinted as a separate pamphlet together with some comments by Shaykh Ḥasanayn Makhlūf, the late grand-mufti of Egypt and quoted by *Ḥabib* Aḥmad Mashhur al-Ḥaddād in *Key to the Garden.*[53] This is what he says: "Praise belongs to God alone. May God bless our master Muḥammad, his Family and Companions, and grant them peace. We know, assent, believe, confess with certainty, and testify that there is no god but God, Alone without partner. He is a Mighty God, a Great King. There is no lord besides Him, and we worship none other than He. He is ancient and Pre-Existent, Eternal and Everlasting. His firstness has no beginning, neither has His lastness any end. He is Solitary, Self-Subsistent, neither begetting nor begotten, matchless, without partner or peer. '*There is nothing that resembles Him, and He is the Hearer, the Seer.*' [42:11]

"And we confess that His holiness (Exalted is He!) renders Him beyond time and space, beyond resembling anything in existence, so that He cannot be encompassed by directions, nor be subject to contingent events. And that He is established on His Throne in the manner which He has described, and in the sense which He has intended, in a manner befitting the might of His Majesty, and the exaltation of His glory and magnificence. And that He (Exalted is He!) is Near to everything in existence, being "*closer to man than his jugular vein.*" [50:16] He is Watchful and Seeing over all things. He is *the Living, the Self-Subsistent, slumber overtakes Him not, nor sleep*; [2:255] He is *the Originator of the heavens and earth; when He decrees a thing He only says to it Be! And it is* [2:117] *God is Creator of all things, and He is Guardian over everything.* [39:62]

"And that He (Exalted be He!) is over all things Powerful, and of all things knower; His knowledge is all-embracing and He keeps count of all things. *Not an atom's weight in the earth or in the sky escapes your Lord.* [10:61] *He knows what goes down into the earth and that which comes forth from it, and what descends from heaven and what ascends into it. He is with you wherever you may be, and God sees well what you do.* [57:4] *He knows what is in the land and the sea. A leaf cannot fall but that He knows it, nor is there a grain amid the darkness of the earth, nor a wet or dry thing, but that is recorded in a clear Book.* [6:59]

"And that he (Exalted be He!) wills existent things, and directs events. And that nothing may exist, whether good or evil, beneficial or harmful, except by His decree and will. Whatever He wills is, whatever He does not, is not. Should all creatures unite to move or halt a single atom in the universe, in the absence of His will, they would be unable to do so.

"And that He (Exalted be He!) is Hearer, Seer, Speaker of a Speech that is pre-existent and does not resemble the speech of creatures. And that the Mighty Qur'ān is His ancient speech, His Book which He sent down upon His Messenger and Prophet Muḥammad (may His blessings and peace be upon him).

"And that He (Transcendent be He!) is Creator of all things and their Provider, Who disposes them as He wills; neither rival nor opponent is there in His realm. He gives to whomsoever He wills and withholds from whomsoever He wills. *He is not questioned about His actions, rather they are questioned* [21:23].

"And that He (Exalted be He!) is Wise in His acts; Just in His decrees, so that no injustice or tyranny can be imaginable on His part, and that no one has any rights over Him.

Should He (Transcendent be He!) destroy all His creatures in the blink of an eye, He would be neither unjust nor tyrannous to them, for they are His dominion and His slaves. He has the right to do as He pleases in His dominion, *and your Lord is not a tyrant to His slave.* [41:46] He rewards His slaves for obeying Him, out of grace and generosity, and punishes them when they rebel, out of His wisdom and justice.

"And that to obey Him is an obligation binding upon His bondsmen, as was made clear through the speech of His messengers (upon them be peace). We believe in every Book sent down by God, and in all of His messengers, His angels, and in destiny, whether good or bad.

"And we testify that Muḥammad is His slave and Messenger, whom He sent to jinn and to mankind, to the Arabs and the non-Arabs, *with guidance and the religion of truth, that he may cause it to prevail over all religion, though the polytheists be averse.* [9:33] And that he delivered the Message, was faithful to his trust, advised the community, did away with grief, and strove for God's sake as is His due, being truthful and trustworthy, supported by authentic proofs and norm-breaking miracles. And that God has made it incumbent upon His slaves to believe, obey, and follow him, and that a man's faith is not acceptable—even should he believe in Him—until he believes in Muḥammad (may God's blessings and peace be upon him and his Family) and in everything that he brought and informed us of, whether of the affairs of this world or the next. This includes faith in the questioning of the dead by Munkar and Nakīr about religion, *tawḥīd* and Prophethood, and in the bliss which is in the grave for those who were obedient, and the torment which it contains for the rebellious.

"And that one should believe in the Resurrection after Death, the gathering of bodies and spirits to stand in the presence of God the Exalted, and in the Reckoning; and that His slaves will be at that time in different states, some being called to account, some being exempted, while others shall enter the Garden without reckoning.

"One should believe in the Scales in which good and evil deeds will be weighed; and in the *Ṣirāṭ*, which is a bridge stretched over the depths of Hell; and in the Pool [*Ḥawḍ*] of our Prophet Muḥammad, may God's blessings and peace be upon him and his Family, the water of which is from the Garden, and from which the believers shall drink before entering the Garden. And in the intercession of the Prophets, followed by the Truthful Saints [*ṣiddīqūn*], and then the scholars, the virtuous [*ṣaliḥūn*] and the other believers. And that the Greatest intercession is the prerogative of Muḥammad (may God's blessings and peace be upon him and his Family). And that the people of *tawḥīd* who have entered the fire shall be taken out of it until not one person in whose heart there lies an atom's weight of faith shall remain in it perpetually. And that the people of polytheism and disbelief shall abide in the Fire perpetually and for evermore, *their suffering shall not be diminished; neither shall they be reprieved* [2:162] and that the believers shall abide in the Garden perpetually and without end, *wherein no tiredness shall befall them, and from which they shall not be expelled.* [15:48] And that the believers shall see their Lord with their eyes, in a way befitting His Majesty and the Holiness of His Perfection.

"And that the Companions of the Messenger of God (may God's blessings and peace be upon him and his family,) were virtuous, that their status was of various ranks, and that they were just, good, and trustworthy. It is not lawful to insult of denigrate any of them. And that the rightful successor [*khalīfa*] to the Messenger of God (may God's blessings and peace be upon him and his Family) was Abū Bakr al-Ṣiddīq, followed by ᶜUmar al-Fārūq, then ᶜUthmān al Shahīd, then ᶜAlī al-Murtaḍā, may God be pleased with them and with all his other Companions, and with those who follow them with excellence until the Day of Judgment, and with us also, by Your mercy, O Most Merciful of Mercifuls!"

As for the ever-vexing question of predestination, the Imām once pointed out that it was one of those that would only be solved in the hereafter. This concept is easy to understand if one keeps in mind that antinomies cannot be resolved by the human mind, which operates on an "either/or" basis, whereas they are resolved in the hereafter by direct contemplation of the union of opposites. This also means that they are resolved by gnostics in this world since they behold the things of the hereafter, while still in this world, with their inward vision. We shall quote some of the Imām's remarks, gleaned from various sources, concerning this question:

"Man intends then moves, while God brings on to pass what He will. The movement may conform to the [Divine] Decree and Destiny *(al-Qaḍā'wal-Qadar)*, in which case the act is completed, or it may not, in which case the act remains undone, while the person remains in possession of his intention, whether good or evil."

"Destinies are spirits, the bodies of which are the acts arising from created beings. Bodies are seen and their nature understood. Spirits, on the other hand, are neither seen nor is their nature understood. So it is with acts and destinies. A man may set out on a journey saying, 'I wish to reach such and such a place,' not knowing what Destiny has in store for him. He may die before reaching his goal or, again in conformity with Destiny, may arrive where he wishes.... In this world destinies are hidden while [secondary] causes are apparent. In the life-to-come destinies are made to appear while [secondary] causes become hidden.

"God has secrets and wisdom in the ordering of [secondary] causes, the interconnection of each of their benefits to the other, and the need each has for the other. This world is that of [secondary] causes, all its affairs depend on them. It is the subject of His saying, "*Be! And it is.*" [36:82] He said, Exalted be He, "*We poured out the rains abundantly, then We split the earth in fissures and therein made the grains to grow and veins, and reeds, and olives and palms, and dense treed gardens, and fruits and pastures, an enjoyment for you and your flocks.*" [80:25-32]. As for *ᶜĀlam al-Amr* (the World of the Command or of essential realities),[54] it is something else; (secondary) causes are inoperant there. Nor is there any need there for the *Kāf* and *Nūn*.[55] Things originate in *al-Qaḍā' wal-Qadar*, but it is the secondary causes that make them manifest. An example of this is the lengthening of life by good works and its shortening by incorrect behavior. Secondary causes and what arise from them are part of the Decree and Destiny. When a person does good works and his life is lengthened or acts in a corrupt manner and it is shortened, he is under decree to act thus and for his life to be as it is in either case.

"On the Guarded Tablet everything is written that is to occur, together with its cause, 'this will happen for this cause, this for that, and so on.' The world, from beginning to end, is managed by angels, not by human beings. Even human beings are managed by angels. Imām al-Ghazālī says that within a human being are seven angels managing his nutrition, one pushes the food to the stomach, another extracts the residues from it, another makes blood flow to the liver, and so on. This is for the lower part of the world, as for the higher part, one drives the cloud, while another carries the water. The running of the earth's affairs and the things of this world are in the hands of human beings only as far as upholding the command of God and His laws are concerned. If you wish God to treat you with His usual gentleness and generosity you should persevere in your usual obedience and acts of worship, for "*God changes not what is in a people, until they change what is in themselves.*" [13:11] And when God wishes something He causes its causes. He thus does not manifest Himself in sheer Omnipotence in this world, but he does so in the next. In this world Omnipotence depends on causes whereas in the next it is the causes which depend on Omnipotence. In this world Omnipotence is hidden in the causes and by it they are made to appear, whereas in the next it is Omnipotence that is manifest and the causes that are hidden in it. He (Transcendent be He!) causes for each thing a cause different from the other, that man should know the extent of His Ability, Exalted be He!"

Another subject that is so emotionally charged no leading scholar ever escapes being questioned about it is that of the Prophet's succession. This was the cause of the splitting of the Muslims early in their history into a *sunni* majority and a *shīᶜa* minority. A Zaydī[56] scholar asked the Imām a number of questions among which was one concerned with this subject. The Imām wrote back saying, "Know that those who rebelled against ᶜAlī, may God be pleased with him, and whom he personally made battle with during his caliphate were of three groups. The first were those who were present on the Day of the Camel, al-Zubayr, Talḥa, and ᶜĀ'isha—may God be pleased with them all—and the people of Basra. They first gave allegiance, then rebelled against him, seeking revenge for the blood of ᶜUthmān, may God be pleased with him. His assassination had neither been carried out, ordered, nor approved by ᶜAlī, may God be pleased with him, but he accepted the allegiance of those who had perpetrated it and did not turn them over, for the good of the faith and to maintain unity among Muslims at that time. These reasons were not understood by the rebels.

The second were those who were at Ṣiffīn, Muᶜāwiya, ᶜAmr ibn al-ᶜĀṣ, and the people of Syria. They had not sworn allegiance to ᶜAlī and they rebelled demanding revenge for ᶜUthmān.

The third were those who were at Nahrawān, the *Khawārij*. They had given him their allegiance and fought with him, then rebelled in rejection of the arbitration that had taken place at Ṣiffīn.

None of those were fought by ᶜAlī, may God be pleased with him, until he had invited them to meet with him for reconciliation and again to accept his authority, and they had refused to do so. In our view they are all people who have overstepped their limits, disputed [what was not theirs], and rebelled with no evident justification or clear right. Those of them who rebelled for disputable reasons are, however, better than those who disputed his authority, because desiring it for themselves. God is more aware of their intentions and inner thoughts. Our safety lies in saying nothing about them, for they are a community that has passed. Our scholars have stated that al-Zubayr and those who were with him and Muᶜāwiya and those who were with him, having exercised their judgment, made the wrong decisions, and are thus excusable. Regardless, the most that it is possible to say about those among the people of *Tawḥid* who pray and pay their *zakāt* but rebel against the head of the state is that they are sinners, and we Muslims are not, in our view, allowed to curse the sinner specifically. We do not consider it to amount to disbelief (*kufr*) to rebel against the leader, nor do we consider it permissible to curse a specified person, except when we know that he died a disbeliever, under no circumstance to be reached by God's mercy, as the Devil for example. Having said that, there is still no virtue in cursing such people. We only allow cursing of sinners, transgressors, and oppressors, in general terms.

As for Ḥasan and Ḥusayn-may God be pleased with them-they were leaders by right and indeed fulfilled the conditions for leadership and were perfectly worthy of it. Ḥasan was sworn allegiance by the 'people of decision' among those who were under Imām ᶜAlī, following the latter's assassination. When Muᶜāwiya and the people of Syria marched against him, he came out to meet them with the people of Iraq. When the two armies drew close to each other, Ḥasan had compassion and pity for the nation, so that God might fulfill that which his grandfather—may blessings and peace be upon him—had said: "This son of mine is a *sayyid*, I hope that through him God the Exalted will bring conciliation between two large groups of Muslims." Ḥasan then deposed himself and pledged his allegiance to Muᶜāwiya, having first imposed some conditions on him. He died—may God be pleased with him—before Muᶜāwiya. The latter designated his son Yazīd as heir, and the people gave him their allegiance, some willingly, others under coercion. Having refused him his allegiance, the people of Iraq wrote to Ḥusayn and requested that he come to them and be their leader. He accepted and set out for Iraq. Yazīd then wrote to his deputy in Basra, ᶜUbaydullāh ibn Ziyād, ordering him to march against Ḥusayn and defeat him. He did so and the people of Iraq allowed for it, although they had at first paid allegiance to Ḥusayn.

Ḥusayn was martyred together with some members of his household—may God be pleased with them all. Those who killed him, those who ordered it, and those who assisted in it we regard as transgressors and violators, may God treat them according to His justice. Yazīd we do not regard as similar to Muᶜāwiya—may God be pleased with him—who was a Companion and who neither neglected his religious obligations nor committed offences. Yazīd, on the other hand, was undoubtedly depraved in that he abandoned his prayers, murdered people, committed adultery, and drank alcohol. His judgment we leave to God the Exalted.

The Imām was once asked, "Did not Muᶜāwiya, who was a Companion, entrust the Caliphate to his son, who then perpetrated these evil things?" He replied, "It has been said that when Muᶜāwiya designated his son to succeed him he said, 'I feel goodness in him, if my intuition comes true, then so be it, but if not, this is nothing but the natural love of a father for his son, and I pray to God not to prolong his life!' When he turned out to be different from what he had thought he did not live long and died, killed in an ugly manner." Then he added, "One should harbor only love and good thoughts for the Companions of the Prophet, may God's blessings and peace be upon him, and refrain from thinking ill of them…."

He is also reported to have remarked: "As for Abū Bakr, it was by consensus. As for ᶜUmar, it was by being designated by Abū Bakr. As for ᶜUthmān, it was by consensus following deliberation (*shūrā*). As for Sayyidunā ᶜAlī, may God be pleased with him, it was by the allegiance of the people of Badr, the Emigrants, and the Helpers. As for

Muᶜāwiya, it was surrendered over to him by al-Ḥasan ibn ᶜAlī, who then gave him his allegiance. As for the others, it was by the sword, tyranny, and aggression, except for ᶜUmar ibn ᶜAbdal-ᶜAzīz, for again it was by consensus and allegiance...."

He was once heard praising the four Caliphs then adding, "Anyone who reflects on the qualities of the Caliphs with perspicacity and complete knowledge will see that the patterns of Abū Bakr and ᶜUthmān are the same, their dominant characters being gentleness and compassion. In opposition to this and similar to each other were Sayyidunā ᶜUmar and Sayyidunā ᶜAlī, in that they showed strength and severity in [the implementation] of God's religion."

Again, when discussing the *Shīᶜa*—which he did freely since there were no native *Shīᶜa* in Hadramawt—and their belief that Sayyidunā ᶜAlī was more worthy of the Caliphate, he said that had he taken over after the Prophet, may blessings and peace be on him, the same events that befell him when he did take over would have occurred to him then. That is, the discord that involved him, the quarrels, and his behavior towards the transgressors were his destiny—for it had been decreed that this would befall him. But Sayyidunā Abū Bakr was accepted by the people, Sayyidunā ᶜAlī among them, for his being the earliest to accept Islam, for his being with the Prophet, may God's blessings and peace be upon him, in the cave,[57] and for his leading the people in prayer during his lifetime, may blessings and peace be upon him.

Chapter 11
SOCIAL INFLUENCE

Definition of the roles of religious and political authorities—the Imām's opinion on the main factors of instability in Muslim society—degeneration of the times—the Imām sets an example for virtuous social behavior.

Since there is no secular domain in Islam and all human affairs are regulated by the Divinely revealed *sharīᶜa*, the religious scholar has always played a pivotal role in Muslim society. Upon him falls the responsibility of "enjoining good and forbidding evil" in the broadest and most detailed manner, to reach every social class and group and to include all their transactions. He must therefore be well acquainted with the circumstances and problems particular to each group and be able to speak to them in the language most accessible to them. The scholar is the judge in legal trials, the mediator and arbiter in commercial and financial disagreements, as well as in familial and marital quarrels. Until recently he was the man most people would consult before making decisions of any consequence.

Religious and political authorities have always been recognized by Muslims as the two main forces shaping society. Imām al Ḥaddād once remarked that "None has cor rupted the people's religious affairs but the scholars, but only after the corruption of their own religious affairs; and none has corrupted the people's worldly affairs but the rulers, but only after the corruption of their own worldly affairs. For when the scholars become corrupt religion follows suit, and when the rulers become corrupt worldly affairs follow suit." This is why every scholar of authority always endeavors to exercise his influence first on fellow scholars and rulers, then on the rest of society. The primacy of religious scholars over political authority was clearly demonstrated by the attitude of the Imām to the sultans and their officials. He never visited the sultan, it was always the sultan who came to him. Sometimes the sultan requested audience and was denied it. The Imām's letters to the sultans were written uncompromisingly and contained not only instructions as to how to conform to *sharīᶜa* but also political and even military advice.

The Imām's views on the main factors of stability in society were briefly stated in the sixth chapter of *Knowledge and Wisdom*:

> The people of this world are of four kinds. Upon these people's virtue and righteousness the world's proper working depends.
>
> The first is the righteous worshipper, the divested renouncer who possesses sound gnosis of God and a profound and penetrating view of religion. The second kind is the scholar of religious sciences, well versed in the knowledge of the Book and *sunna*, who practices what he knows, teaches it to others, is of good counsel, enjoins good, forbids evil, does not compromise in matters of religion, and fears no blame. The third kind is the ruler who is just and equitable, whose outward conduct and inner self are good, and whose policies show rectitude. The fourth kind is the virtuous man of wealth, whose fortune is large, licit, and spent in good ways.

> He uses their wealth to comfort the weak and the destitute and fulfill the needs of the needy. He accumulates wealth only for this purpose, for the goodness and nobility of such behavior.
>
> In opposition to each of these kinds of people are others who resemble them outwardly but differ in meaning and in reality. Opposed to the righteous man of worship is the confused deceitful Sufi; opposed to the scholar who practices what he knows is the depraved compromising scholar; opposed to the just ruler is the tyrant of iniquitous conduct, whose policies and management are evil and unjust; and opposed to the wealthy man of virtue is the inequitable rich man who accumulates wealth illicitly, withholding it when it should be spent, and spending it when it should not. The latter four [kinds] are the cause of the world's corruption and instability, the confusion in people's affairs, and their abandoning of the right ways.

The Imām's perspective is obviously based on his concern to preserve as much as possible and for as long as possible the pattern of behavior and social interaction laid by *sharīᶜa* and practiced by the earliest Muslims. His acute awareness of the downward slide of Muslim society away from the norm laid down by the Prophet's example and that of his Companions brought about such bitter comments as the following: "The people of this time have forgotten God by neglecting His rights, He therefore subjected them to that which keeps them pre-occupied. When they make *duᶜā'*, He does not answer them and the angels do not recognize their voices, for they are not accustomed to hear them doing *dhikr* or any other act of worship...." The Imām also said, "Do not think that the trials of this time will abate.

No, whenever you see a sedition that has abated it will only be like a fire smouldering underneath the ashes, not extinct but only hidden. For people are overpowered by their love of the world, of wealth and eminence. He who loves wealth and eminence can only expect himself to remain subject to temptation until such time as he breaks free of them. The one who says he fears neither shame nor flame, consider him not human."[58]

The ineluctable nature of this degeneration was also clear to him, for had the Prophet, may God's blessings and peace be upon him, not said: "No time will come upon you but that the following will be more evil, until you meet with your Lord."[59] And the Imām himself once stated that "Light will gradually disappear and darkness will gradually increase until the Hour comes." Within this context and that of what was practically feasible he did his best to slow down the pace of the downward slide and in so doing left his mark on all segments of society. His influence was shaped by his thorough knowledge of *sharīᶜa*, history and the people, and both his powerfully charismatic personality and exemplary behavior. For he was a man who practiced what he taught and his efforts were along the lines stated in *"Al-Daᶜwa al-Tāmma"* where he divides society, from the perspective of "enjoining good and forbidding evil," into eight segments. He places the scholars at the summit of the hierarchy, followed by the Sufis, the rulers, the merchants and craftsmen, the poor, the dependents such as women and children, those complying with *sharīᶜa,* those transgressing its limits, and finally those who did not surrender to God. He defines as clearly as possible each group's rights and duties and the consequences of neglecting them.

As for scholars, according to the Imām, their duties are to acquire knowledge solely for the sake of God, not for worldly benefit, to seek only the kind of knowledge that is profitable to themselves and the people, to avoid polemics and sterile debates, to practice what they learn with sincerity and constantly teach it to others, and finally to "enjoin good and forbid evil" gently, wisely, and fearlessly.

His view of the duties of rulers is that they should model themselves on the rightly-guided leaders of the past, acquire what is for them indispensable religious knowledge, uphold with reverence the tenets of Islam, fight corruption at all levels, uphold the statutory rulings of *sharī*^{c}*a*, behave with propriety towards their subjects (that is, with compassion for the weak, the destitute, and those subject to injustice) and with rigor towards the oppressors and transgressors. Their doors should be kept open for those wishing to present their cases. They should appoint only religiously upright people to positions of responsibility and they should respect the possessions of their subjects.

The Imām's behavior towards his family and those around him was a model to be copied by those wishing to improve their own. He was a constant living reminder of how God and His Messenger wish a community to behave. Whenever a youngster from among his relatives—however distant—became orphaned, he was always the first to claim and take him or her into his family, so that there were constantly orphans being raised in his house with his own children. He inquired about poor families, especially widows, and extended regular assistance to them, especially during feast days and other seasons. The workers on his plantations were under instruction to allow strangers, travelers, and the poor to eat from them freely. Whenever he hired workers for a task he always paid them more than he had promised and more than the current worth of the work on the market, so as to make sure they departed contented and at peace. His house was ever full of guests and his table always ready to receive more, especially in Ramaḍān. He and his disciples were living examples of how one should be patient and serene in times of hardship and generous in times of affluence, how to be tolerant of each other's weaknesses, and how to carefully nurture their ties of kinship. He spoke to each person according to his or her understanding and taught them how to solve their problems according to the prophetic wisdom, so that this pattern would become to them a permanent acquisition to be used whenever necessary without recourse to his personal intervention with every new situation.

Chapter 12
THE POLE

Who is the Pole? The Circle of Sainthood—attributes of the Pole—recognition by the other saints of the Imām's supremacy.

"Poleship," writes the Imām, "means lordship. This is why the term Pole is used analogically for whoever possesses lordship over the men of a particular spiritual station or state. There is thus a "Pole of the People of Contentment" *(Quṭb al Rāḍīn),* and so on. The "Possessor of the Degree of Supreme Veracity" is called *al-Quṭb al-Ghawth* to avoid any confusion arising from an analogical use of the term *Quṭb*. To elaborate further would require us to mention the inward states of the men of the "Circle of Sainthood" *(Dā*ᶜ*irat al-Wilāya),* their characteristics, the differences within each rank, and other such things the full knowledge of which belongs by right only to the *Quṭb*, the *Ghawth*, who encompasses all their ranks and whose rank and state comprehend every single one of theirs. As for other saints, they know about those who are of equal or lesser ranks. They are aware of those above them, but have no full knowledge of them. On the whole, these are questions which can be answered satisfactorily only by contemplative vision and unveiling."

The Circle of Sainthood that the Imām mentions is that conference of saints described in the *ḥadith* transmitted by Imām Abū-Nuᶜaym in *Ḥilyat'al-Awliyā'*, which states that there are, at any one time, three hundred saints on earth whose hearts resemble that of Adam, forty resembling Moses, seven Abraham, five Gabriel, three Michael, and one Seraphiel (Isrāfīl)." Al-Yāfe[c]ī quotes this *ḥadith* in *Rawḍ al-Rayāḥīn* then remarks that, the one who resembles the heart of Seraphiel is the *Quṭb* and *Ghawth* and "his position among saints is that of the point at the center of the circle. By him the good functioning of the world is sustained." These passages were quoted by Imām al Ḥaddād in answer to a question concerning the Pole. He adds, "As for the *Quṭb*, the *Ghawth*, he is one in each time. He is the all-comprehensive *Fard*, and is known among the People as the viceregent (*Khalīfa*), and the Perfect Man *(al-Insān al-Kāmil).* Also attributed to him are the titles of *Ṣāḥib al-Ṣiddīqiyya al-Kubrā wal-Wilāya al-[c]Uẓmā* (The Possessor of the Degree of Supreme Veracity and Greatest Sainthood)." He also said in answer to another question, "He is a beloved slave around whom everything revolves. His sign is that he is awe-inspiring, feared by the tyrants and the sons of this world but loved by every believer. His sign is also that he has no inclination whatsoever to choose other than God, and his mind is never disturbed by whatever is happening in the universe; were he to see the earth in full blossom, then look again to find that everything has disappeared, his thoughts would remain unperturbed in the certain knowledge that none other than God has made and destroyed it."

In a well known poem, Imām al Ḥaddād describes the Pole as a master whose qualities are humility, reverence, circumspection, piety, and detachment from created things. His behavior is *sharī[c]a*, his spiritual state is *ḥaqīqa*, and his rank is slavehood or *[c]Ubūda*. He is benevolent and compassionate towards all creatures and looks after all things with gentleness. His sea is supplied from the Ocean of

Oceans (meaning the light of the Prophet, may God's blessings and peace be upon him). When these verses were sung before him he said, "This is the description that comprehends the attributes of the Pole, so that those who read it will know that anyone not conforming to it is not a Pole." Similar descriptions can be read in his poems in praise of Shaykh ᶜAbdal-Qādir, al-Faqīh al-Muqaddam, and al-ᶜAydarūs, all of whom were undisputed masters of their times. And it is to these supreme masters that the Imām was likened by the gnostics of his own time, one of whom said "Sayyid ᶜAbdallāh possesses the attributes of the great ones such as Shaykh ᶜAbdal-Qādir al-Jīlānī and in him the secrets of the ancestors have become outwardly manifest." Another said that he possessed "sublime determination and a superior state comparable to that of Abū Yazīd al-Bisṭāmī." He then urged the people not to allow the opportunity to slip past them saying, "Delight, therefore, O people of Hadramawt, in sitting with Sayyid Abdallāh and in his having been raised amongst you, for he is God's *khalīfa* on earth."

It has been said that the Poles were of three kinds, the Pole of Sciences, such as the Proof of Islam al-Ghazālī, the Pole of Spiritual States, such as Abū Yazīd al-Bistāmī, and the Pole of Spiritual Stations, such as Shaykh ᶜAbdal-Qādir. Imām Abul-ᶜAbbās al-Mursī is also reported to have said, "Al-Junayd was the Pole of knowledge, Sahl the Pole of Stations, and Abū Yazīd the Pole of States.' This was confirmed by Imām al-Ḥaddād when he said, "The one who excels in his own art and surpasses everyone else is the Pole of this art. It is said, for instance, that al-Ghazālī was the Pole of Sciences, Sahl the Pole of stations, and so on.' Sayyid Aḥmad ibn Zayn al-Ḥabashī stated that Imām al-Ḥaddād was the supreme master of masters and that he had united in himself the attributes of all the previous saints, adding that this was seen by him in contemplative vision, meaning that it was no mere mental conclusion. This is why Imām al-Ḥaddād said, "Our rank cannot be shouldered by a single man, and we shall have to divide it, before our death, among a number of people." The Imām was able to give further precisions concerning the Pole in brief statements given on many different occasions. He said, "The Pole must be a known man. If he does not qualify for outward renown he must deputize someone who does." And, "A woman may attain to the [spiritual] rank of the *Abdāl*, but she will not be one of them [in title]. A woman may be neither a Pole nor one of the *Abdāl*." And he suggested some limits to the absolutist statements about the Pole that one often hears. In one of his letters he writes, "Now as regards the fact that nothing reaches the people of the Circle except with the knowledge of the Pole, this is correct as concerns general secrets and that which relates to the function that they are entrusted with for the good of the world." And further on in the same letter, "As for your saying that the Pole's contemplative station is that of the Presence of the Name Allāh and that he is therefore called ᶜAbd-Allāh, God's Slave, this was stated by Shaykh ibn ᶜArabī with lengthy elaborations. It is correct as far as he is concerned and we concede it to him. But this statement is limiting and too narrowly specific, and there is some ambiguity to it."

As concerns his own investiture with this supreme function, Imām al-Ḥaddād is reported to have said in his youth, "I have been promised the Degree of Supreme Veracity." Later on a man came to him to relate a dream vision where he had seen the angels, the Prophets, and the saints, all gathered for a momentous event, after which he was informed, still in the dream, that they had just invested Sayyid

ʿAbdallāh with the function of the Pole. Hearing this, the Imām promised to invest him with the *Khirqa* if his dream were to come true. A few days later he did perform the investiture, which led the man to conclude that his dream had indeed come true. It was said at the time that this had happened at the death of Sayyid Muḥammad ibn ʿAlawī of Makka, who had been the Pole of his time and from whom Imām al-Ḥaddād had inherited this function when his *Khirqa* had reached him in Tarīm on the day of the *sayyid*'s death. This was 1070 H., and the Imām was 26 years old. A few days later, as the Imām was walking home in the company of Shaykh Muḥammad Bā-Jubayr, having visited the Bashshār cemetery, he said to him, "O Shaykh Muḥammad, your *ḥabīb* has been in the station of the Pole for three days now." And to others the Imām related that he had seen an unnamed person come to him in a dream and say, "You are the Pole, the *Ghawth*, you are the master of the time, " then the person cried out as loudly as he could, "I testify that there is no god other than God, that Muḥammad is the Messenger of God, and that ʿAbdallāh ibn ʿAlawī al-Ḥaddād is the Pole." "Then," continued the Imām, "he split my chest open painlessly, took out things which I did not see, as if he were emptying it in order to fill it with other things. I remembered there the splitting of the Chosen One's chest, may God's blessings and peace be upon him, and its filling with knowledge and wisdom. Dream visions are one part of prophethood." Here the Imām was not revealing this dream as proof that he was the Pole, since dreams cannot prove anything, but rather he used it as an indirect statement to inform some of his disciples of his state. And he once said, "The spirits greet me with *salām* every day at sunrise, they call me from all four directions.... Those calling from before me are the saints, those from the right are those who love and believe in us, those from the left are those who deny or object to us, those from behind are those who have turned away from us." This vision was said by the gnostics to be the prerogative of the *khalīfa* and this was another indirect way for the Imām to reveal something of his secret.

Sayyid Aḥmad al-Hunduwān and Sayyid ᶜAli ibn ᶜAbdallāh al-ᶜAydarūs were two great gnostic *shaykhs* who knew Imām al-Ḥaddād well. The Imām had said of the first that he knew of no one who was nearer to the Degree of Supreme Veracity, he was one of the two Imāms on the right and left of the Pole, one of whom succeeds him at his death; the second he often praised, even in his poems. The testimony of such people is therefore highly relevant as concerns the rank of the Imām. Their respect and reverence for him are sufficient testimony, but they also stated on repeated occasions their conviction. Al-ᶜAydarūs once said, "Sayyid Abdallāh al-Ḥaddād is the sultan of the house of ᶜAbū ᶜAlawī in these times." And al-Hunduwān said, "None has reached the station of Sayyidī ᶜAbdallāh so as to be able to describe it." This knowledge was also common among many saints who had never physically met the Imām. A Madina man born of Moroccan parents, known as Abul-Tayyib al-Maghribī, went to visit his uncles in Morocco and there heard of a saint of great renown, whom people traveled from far away places to visit. He went to visit him and as soon as he set eyes on him the thought occurred to him that he must be the Pole. The *shaykh* immediately turned to him saying, "O my son, I am not the Pole of the day, the Pole of the day is Sayyid ᶜAbdallāh al-Ḥaddād in the Yemen." And Imām al-Ḥaddād himself once stated unequivocally, "I am the unique one of my epoch and I am thoroughly well hidden." And he said, "We used to ask from everyone, now everyone asks from us." Once as he was sitting in the Hujayra mosque he said, "I am the master of my time and none may oppose me in that; those who do I dissolve just, as water dissolves salt." This last sentence refers to inward not outward opposition, since outward opposition was frequent and always forgiven, in conformity with the *sunna*. And when one of his disciples sought his permission to sit with the scholars and saints of Tarīm, he granted it, then added, "Know that the saints of this time are all fed with our light."

Another disciple by the name of ᶜAbdal-Raḥmān Bā-Raqaba, a gnostic saint of ᶜAlawī descent, once met a dervish as he was standing before the Kaᶜba in Makka. His heart told him this was a man of God and he felt an upsurge of love for him to which the man responded by saying, "I love you in God!" Sayyid ᶜAbdal-Raḥmān replied, "So do I." Then he asked him from whence he came. He replied that he hailed from Morocco and was a decendant of Imām al-Ḥasan. On being asked the same question Sayyid ᶜAbdal-Raḥmān said, "from Tarīm." Hearing this, the dervish immediately asked, "Do you know Sayyid ᶜAbdallāh al-Ḥaddād? "How can I not know him," asked the *sayyid,* "when he and I live in the same town?" Noticing how intensely interested the dervish had become, he inquired, "Do you also know him?" "We know each other in spirit," he replied, then added that Imām al-Ḥaddād was the Pole of the Circles, their center, and that he had united in himself knowledge, sanctity, and the honor of belonging to the house of Prophecy. This, he stated, was very rare indeed, that all three attributes be united in one person. He also mentioned that he had a great desire to see him, and then asked the *sayyid* to convey his *salām* to him once he returned home. On his first meeting with the Imām, having returned to Hadramawt, Sayyid ᶜAbdal-Raḥmān forgot to convey the message, until the Imām asked him, "Did you hear anything concerning us over there? Has anyone said anything about us?" Only then did he remember and, in later years, recounted the incident firstly as indicating the Imām's rank as Pole of his time and secondly as evidence of his ability to maintain constant awareness of his disciples' activities however remote in space they might be.

Chapter 13
THE *ḤAJJ* JOURNEY

Predictions concerning the pilgrimage of the Imām—tyranny of the governor—traveling to the Ḥajj—Shaykh Ḥusayn Bā-Faḍl's hospitality—rites of the pilgrimage—karāmāt in Makka—visit to Madina—return to Makka—spiritual openings.

As a youngster, Imām ᶜAbdallāh was told by one of his maternal uncles who was something of a *majdhūb* that on such and such a year he would go on *ḥajj*, that when he would reach a certain location a mule would be brought for him to ride into Makka and that the people of Makka would come out to meet him. He also told him that he would travel to Madina and that at another location which he specified, God would pour upon him "light without intermediary." In effect, the Imām went on *ḥajj* only once in his lifetime, in the year 1079 H. and returned to Hadramawt by way of the Yemen in 1080 H.

As he was preparing to set out on his journey, the people of Tarīm came to him to complain about the tyranny of the area governor. This man had visited the Imām on many occasions, each time to be admonished and urged to treat the people with more compassion. He seemed impervious to the Imām's advice, however, and it was once reported to the Imām that he had said, "Sayyid ᶜAbdallāh wants me to be like ᶜUmar ibn ᶜAbdal-ᶜAzīz, the just caliph." These words greatly angered the Imām, who said, "These days, should a perfect man wish to be as just as ᶜUmar ibn ᶜAbdal-ᶜAzīz in his own house, let alone elsewhere, he would be opposed by everything, even by his own clothes." To the people who had come complaining he responded, "By the time I return from *ḥajj* he shall have died." When he reached the port of Aden he said to his companions, "The people of the Intermediary Realm have complained to me about the governor's injustice. God has aimed two arrows at him, he is now wounded." They set sail and once in mid-sea, the Imām summoned them for a funeral prayer. They prayed for that governor the "prayer for the absent" (*ṣalāt'al-ghā'ib*). None of them dared question him about it, but they recorded in writing the date of the event and when they eventually returned to Hadramawt, were able to ascertain that the man had indeed died on that day. This was one of the rare occasions when the Imām let something transpire of his hidden function.

The Imām set out from Tarīm towards the southern port of al-Shiḥr. The caravan halted in a valley and began to unload. It was a dry evening and the sky was clear. Then the Imām said, "Reload!" which they did and began to move out of the valley. Suddenly there was lighting and thunder then rain poured down. "I see a place over there," said the Imām, pointing with his hand at a place no one else was able to see in the dark. "Rise!" he said. They rose out of the valley, halted, lit fires, and looking down in the valley, they saw that the rain had flooded it. They resumed their journey and by midday while crossing another valley, felt so tired that they decided to halt for a rest. The Imām refused to allow this saying, "Keep going!" They kept going, and having crossed that valley, were allowed by the Imām to camp in another. A short while later a flood of torrential force swept over the first valley, uprooting the trees.

As they approached al-Shiḥr, one the Imām's disciples sought his permission to precede them in order to arrange for suitable quarters. The Imām refused, saying, "Be courteous with us! We have come out with God, Exalted is He. We ask none other than Him and we arrange nothing for ourselves. The first man that we meet shall be our man." A *sayyid* by the name of Ḥusayn met them. He was from the house of al-Saqqāf, with whom they had no previous acquaintance. He invited them to his house where they found that he had provided the house to receive them. The lanterns had been lit, dinner was being prepared, and the servants were making ready the guest rooms. As coffee was served, their host informed them that a ship that was about to set sail would be delayed for their sake to carry them to Hudayyida, the main port of Northern Yemen, and that they would accept no fare for the trip. The Imām remained in al-Shiḥr for three days in the course of which he visited the saints in the area, both the living and the dead. Among the living was a grandson of the illustrious Shaykh Abū Bakr ibn Sālim, a high-ranking saint in his own right who remarked that the Imām's visit to the town was a great gift from God. He also wished to inform the people in the mountains surrounding the port, so that they may come down to look at him, for as he said, "To look at him is a great gain."

The Imām interrupted his journey briefly in Aden to visit the tomb of another illustrious ᶜAlawī, Shaykh Abū Bakr al-ᶜAydarūs, on whose poem of gnosis he had written, seven years before, an illuminating commentary and included it in *Gifts for the Seeker*.

In Hudayyida, they transferred to another ship where they happened to find a man who sang Sufi poems. They asked the Imām to allow the man to chant them some poems and he permitted it. No sooner did he start than ᶜAbdal-

Raḥmān Sharāḥīl, one of his close disciples, found himself wondering at the display somewhat critically. To the company's surprise, the Imām bid the singer to stop, and then he said, "This kind of audition is *ḥarām* for most people except for gnostics and those whom they have taken over." Then, pointing his hand at Sharāḥīl, he added, "One of our companions has had a reprehensible thought." At this four men rose towards Sharāḥīl, reproaching him his discourtesy in humiliating words. To expose disciples in such situations is unusual indeed for masters. Only when they wish to teach a promising disciple a permanent lesson and can find no other way to do it would they risk such a tactic. It is to Sharāḥīl's credit that the Imām behaved thus with him, for it meant that he knew for certain that he was not one to take offence and would be able to subdue his ego and heed the lesson thereafter. In effect, as Sharāḥīl recounted the incident in later years, he stated that he repented there and then and since then no further thoughts of this kind had bothered him.

The Makka Gate in Jeddah as it looked
over one hundred years ago.

Finally, the Imām and his party of about ten people reached Jeddah, a very small coastal town in those days.

He received many letters. Everyone who had learnt of his arrival wrote to him inviting him to be his guest during his sojourn in Makka. One of his disciples again sought his permission to precede him into Makka to arrange for lodgings, but he again refused, saying that they were God's guests and whatever He had arranged for them they would gladly accept. So it was that they accepted the invitation contained in the very first letter that reached them, which was that of Shaykh Ḥusayn Bā-Faḍl, a man of Hadramī origin, indicated by the typical Bā preceding his name. He wrote to the Imām saying, "I have a house which I have built but allowed no one to inhabit before you. My wish was that you would be the first to inhabit it."

They entered Makka in the month of Dhul-Ḥajja, the people of the sanctuary came out in force to meet the Imām, bringing along a mule for him to ride into the city, thereby fulfilling the first part of his uncle's prophecy and providing the Divine sign that the second, and more important part, was also to be fulfilled in due course.

Bā-Faḍl said, "I beg you never refrain from informing us the moment you need anything." To which the Imām replied, "Should a need arise for a created being there is none worthier than you that we should inform, and we are in your home. However, should God, Transcendent be He, fulfill all the needs, there shall remain nothing to be said. Know this and act accordingly."

As the pilgrims in these days usually did, the Imām and his party carried with them many provisions and oncc in the house, they said to Bā-Faḍl, "Strain yourself not on account of us, for we have with us everything that we need." The host, intending not to miss the opportunity to be of

The area of Makka where the Blessed Prophet was born.

Bāb al-Ṣafā, the gate marking the Hill of Ṣafā in Makka.

service to one of the most illustrious saints of the Prophetic House, replied that since they were in his house they must accept his hospitality on that first night. By this he meant supper, which he did indeed provide in the most ample manner. The next morning he arranged for mounts for every one of them to be waiting in front of the house in order to carry them into the city. He then continued to anticipate their every need and arrange for all their meals until, when the time came for them to depart for Madina, he hired the necessary mounts and settled the caravaneer's fare in advance to take them there and back.

There was a constant stream of visitors to the Imām's quarters in Makka. No person of any consequence failed to visit him and seek his *baraka*. He received them affably, as was his custom, and delighted them by inquiring about their names and ancestry. With one particular visitor, however, he deliberately omitted to ask the usual questions. The man who seems to have had a spiritual rank of some importance was offended by the Imām's disinterest and thought, "Does not this *sayyid* fear to be dispossessed?" (This refers to the power of the higher saint to dispossess someone of lower rank of his spiritual state, should he be guilty of discourtesy or any other offence punishable in their own special code.) The Imām immediately replied, "Dispossession is an existing reality, but God has safeguarded us from it."

Some of his visitors knew him by reputation; others were providentially led to his doorstep. ᶜAbdal-Raḥmān Bā-Sharāḥīl related how the Imām once told him to sit at the door and allow no one in so that he could take his midday nap, the *qaylūla,* which is thc *sunna* of the Prophet, may God's blessings and peace be upon him. There then came a man dressed as a merchant who stopped before the house and inquired about a person who seems to have lived thereabout in the past. Then the man took a deep breath and said, "I smell the breath of a gnostic!" ᶜAbdal-Raḥmān provided him with some information about the Imām which led the man to insist that he must see him, urging him to obtain permission for him to enter. As this conversation proceeded, the Imām sensed the man's presence and called upon him to enter, which he did, showing great deference and courtesy. He informed the *shaykh* that he was from Baghdad, divulged his secret to him, and asked to be granted the *ijāza* and the *khirqa*. The Imām granted both requests, following which ᶜAbdal-Raḥmān saw light shining forth from the man. As he watched him depart he was overcome with grief, that this stranger had been given so much in such a brief time. The Imām turned toward him saying, "None ever receives the things of the men of God and their gifts unless providentially guided, with sincerity and serious efforts. If your wish is to triumph and reach your goal, worship Him openly and secretly. It is not profitable to [merely] keep the company [of the great men of God] even if assiduously and intimately; nevertheless, those who do so, if sincere, never fail."

In later years the Imām was to say that when he had gone on *ḥajj,* his wish was to meet with two men—two oceans, as he described them, one a master of exoteric knowledge and the other a master of reality. He had questions to ask for which he had so far found no answer. Therefore, whenever he heard of someone who was a master of *ḥadith* or of exoteric sciences, he sought to meet with him. He never finished his quest, however, for he was always met with great deference and told: "It is we who wish to learn and benefit from you," or, "We request to be allowed to take from you and read in your presence." Whenever he met with those considered to be possessed of inward knowledge, he was invariably asked to "give them the path and invest them with the *khirqa*." It may seem odd at first sight that the Imām was searching for those who would provide him with answers to his questions despite being the supreme scholar and saint of his time. One must remember, however, that Moses, may peace be upon him, despite being a major Messenger of God, experienced the same situation in the company of al-Khidr, and such is the state of all created beings that none of them ever reaches absolute perfection.

During his sojourn in Makka the Imām did what Muslims do. He circumambulated the Kaᶜba, kissed the Black Stone, drank from the well of Zamzam, and visited the Maᶜlā cemetery.

The well of Zamzam which sprang miraculously to save Ismāᶜīl, may peace be upon him, and his mother Hājar from death by thirst, was said by the Prophet, may God's blessings and peace be upon him, to be "good for whatever it is drunk for."[59] The Imām explained this, "It means that the one who drinks it for a sickness, God cures it, or for another purpose, God fulfills it, because the original purpose had been to succor. By it God succored Ismāᶜīl, may peace be upon him. The Imāms have tried it for [obtaining] their requests and found this to be true, as he [the Prophet] had said, may blessings and peace be upon him. It needs [firmness of] intention and sincerity, however; it is not for everyone."

As for the Maᶜlā, it is the main Makkan cemetery. There lies the lady Khadīja, the Prophet's first wife, the perfect saint, as well as many of the Companions and Followers, and in the left hand corner as soon as one enters the gate of the cemetery there is a square area reserved for the ᶜAlawīs. The Imām also visited the Shubayka cemetery, particularly to visit Sayyid ᶜAbdallāh ibn Muḥammad Bīlfaqīh. The first time he went there, however, he said that Sayyid ᶜAbdallāh was not there in his grave and he turned around and left immediately. The next time he visited that cemetery he sat for a long time, saying that the *sayyid* was now in his grave, he therefore took his time and made a long *duᶜā'*.

Then it was time to move to ᶜArafāt, the most important day for the thousands of pilgrims who had come from the four corners of the earth for the meeting with their Lord's mercy and forgiveness. Bā-Sālim, one of the Imām's companions said, "When I spread *sayyidī's* rug in the mosque of Namira, a man who looked Turkish appeared and sat on this rug. The mosque became exceedingly crowded, and I remained perplexed by the man still sitting on the rug but did not dare speak to him. When the *shaykh* arrived the man was suddenly no longer there to be seen. I then realized that he had been guarding the rug lest someone else should sit on it. After the *shaykh* left the mosque, and arrived at his tent, a man with the looks of a wandering dervish, whose name was ᶜAbdal-Khāliq al-Maghribī, entered behind him, greeted him with *salām*, and then sat down and behaved with great courtesy. The *shaykh* welcomed him warmly and said, "So you are one of the People of the Secret (*ahl al-sirr*) whom I have asked God to show me and three of whom He did indeed show me?" The dervish replied affirmatively. He had visited Hadramawt in the past and was thus known to the Imām. He was said to be one of the People of the Step (*ahl al-khaṭwa)*—those saints capable of traveling instantaneously from one location to another simply by putting the right foot forward and saying "*bismillāh*." The man himself confirmed this saying that he had indeed come to *ḥajj* from Madina using the "Step" and planned to return that same night to Makka and then to Madina in the same manner. He said to the Imām, "We shall see you in Makka if you go to Makka tonight, otherwise the meeting shall be in Madina."

The Imām and his party then left their tent to head for the Mount of Mercy, that same mount beneath which the Prophet, may God's blessings and peace be upon him, had stood on his she-camel during the farewell pilgrimage to deliver his final address. The day was a Friday and the group remained engrossed in *du*ᶜ*ā'* until after the sun had disappeared. A man whom they did not know rose to his feet from behind the Imām and gave the call for the sunset prayer. He then had the Imām come forward to lead the prayer. As soon as this was over another man rose to his feet and cried out very loudly, "O people of the concourse, this is the Pole, he is performing his *ḥajj* amongst you, so thank God the Exalted!"

The Imām did not return to Makka that night, which was the night of the ᶜĪd, but remained in Muzdalifa and afterwards, Minā. Once the days of Minā were over, he returned to the holy city to again receive his visitors, dispense of his knowledge and blessings, and teach by his words and by his example.

In Muḥarram of 1080 H., a certain *sharīf* Barakāt approached Imām al-Ḥaddād in the *ḥijr*, the semi-circular enclosure facing the northern wall of the Kaᶜba, where Ismāᶜīl and Hājar are buried, and asked him for his *du*ᶜ*ā'* (for a request which he did not specify). The Imām complied and prayed for him. After his departure he commented, "The *sharīf* has asked us to become governor and God has granted it to us." And effectively, on the 13th of Dhul-Ḥajja in the year 1082, the sultan's troops assisted the *sharīf* in gaining control of the Hijāz and becoming its governor.

Two other *karāmāt* were reported by ᶜAbdal-Raḥmān Sharāḥīl to have occurred in those days. The first was when,

Al-Khayf Mosque in Minā. The white dome marks the place where the Prophet had his tent erected.

The Namira Mosque at ᶜArafat one hundred years ago.

The spot in ᶜArafāt where the Prophet stood on the Farewell Pilgrimage.

as he was sitting with the Imām one evening, he felt in his heart a desire for dates, at which the Imām turned to him saying, "How weak is your aspiration, could you not have desired something better? The dates are now on their way to us!" No sooner had he spoken than Shaykh Bā-Faḍl knocked on the door. It had not been his custom to visit the Imām at such hours and he explained it by saying that just as he was about to retire, the thought of the dates persistently bothered him, and he felt he had to take them to the Imām henceforth. The Imām then said to Sharāḥīl, "Here, fulfil your desire, but beware of such thoughts! We have not come to Makka for any such thing. Raise your aspiration to your Lord and invoke God the Exalted in abundance." The second *karāma* was that the Imām bid him return to Hadramawt, at which he was greatly distressed since it meant that he would miss visiting the Prophet, may God's blessings and peace be upon him, in Madina in the Imām's company. He complied, however, and immediately set out on his way back. When he arrived home he was told that his father had died eight days before, and he found his mother and sisters in the throes of a severe illness, unable to look after one another and with no one around to care for them.

The Imām then decided that the time had come to visit Madina. On the last Friday of Muḥarram, just prior to his departure, he led the morning prayer before the Kaᶜba and recited *sūras* al-Sajda and al-Insān.

In Madina he met Shaykh ᶜAbdal-Khāliq al-Maghribī again and was invited to his home. "We had thought him to be a man of divestment (*mutajarrid*)," said the Imām, meaning one of those whose station was one of total reliance upon God's provision and who therefore owned nothing of the world except the clothes they wore, "but we found him

Madina in 1907

to have a house and servants." The Imām added, "He asked me to which school I belonged," meaning which of the four schools of jurisprudence, "and my conviction was that my school was the Book and *sunna* and I wished to tell him so, but for fear of objections I said, 'My school is Shāfi^{c}ī.' He said, 'No, your school is the Book and *sunna.*' I said, 'All my ancestors belonged to the school of Imām al-Shāfi^{c}ī,' and he said, 'Why do you say that you are Shāfi^{c}ī? Your school is but the Book and *sunna.*'" This was one of three men whom Imām al-Ḥaddād said had been able to read his thoughts. One of the others was a man in Ta^{c}iz of the Yemen. When they visited him they were accompanied by a man who claimed to be a *sharīf* but about whose claim the Imām had some doubts. The *shaykh* they were visiting said outrightly, "The man is not a *sharīf.*"

These doors open onto the place where the Prophet's home stood and where he is buried—now included within the confines of the Prophet's Mosque in Madina.

Throughout his stay in Madina, the Imām had daily reading sessions in which his book *al-Naṣā'iḥ al-Dīniyya* was read before the chamber of the Prophet, may God's blessings and peace be upon him. He had written parts of it before setting off for *ḥajj* and he had reached precisely the chapter on *ḥajj*. He had intended to complete it in the course of his journey but the large number of visitors prohibited him from doing so.

Shaykh Ḥusayn Bā-Faḍl fell seriously ill and, because it was revealed to the Imām by way of unveiling that his life was coming to an end, he gathered their companions and requested them to grant him parts of their own lives. The first to volunteer was Sayyid ᶜUmar Amīn who declared that he was willing to give away eighteen days of his life. He was followed by all the others, including the Imām. They added up this period and wrote down the total that had been offered. The Imām took the paper and headed for the Prophet's tomb. He stood there with great reverence and humility, requesting his intercession in that matter. When he came out of the mosque they could see that he was greatly relieved. "God has accepted our petition and answered us," he said, "God erases what He will and confirms." Shaykh Ḥusayn Bā-Faḍl recovered. Later, when the Imām had returned to Tarīm and the time granted to Bā-Faḍl had run out, he informed his companions that their Makkan friend was soon to die. Shortly afterward, news arrived from Makka that Bā-Faḍl had indeed passed away.

They were visited in Madina by a man from the house of al-ᶜAmūdī who had been a close companion of Sayyid Muḥammad ibn ᶜAlawī al-Saqqāf. So attached to the *sayyid* was he that when the latter died, he remained sitting near his grave for a full year, rising only to perform his ablutions, pray, or to sleep. Then he saw a dream vision that led him to leave Makka for Madina where he began to read the Aphorims of Shaykh Abū Madian before the Imām. Soon afterward his voice became hoarse and he said to the Imām, "I fear that Sayyid Muḥammad does not like my reading before you." To which the Imām replied, "No, we and Sayyid Muḥammad and the superior ones among the *sayyids* are one and the same." This idea was further explained by the Imām on another occasion when he said that they were all outwardly separate but inwardly united. This is something still readily observable among the ᶜAlawī *sayyids* today; they always impart the very strong impression that they are a single spirit in different bodies and personalities.

The Imām remained in Madina for forty days. He had intended to leave earlier but on the eve of his intended departure he saw in his sleep that he was leaving the house he was staying in and heading for the Prophet's mosque. "A woman stood in my way and wished to kiss my hand," said the Imām. "I withdrew my hand into my sleeve then gave it to her and she kissed it and then said, 'How like the hand of Sayyid Muḥammad ibn ᶜAlawī this hand is!' Then she added, 'Your ancestor the Prophet, may God's blessings and peace be upon him, says: stay in Madina, do not leave it.' And there was a man behind me saying, 'This is Compassion,' meaning by this Madina itself, since this is one of its names. I was pleased by the name, Compassion auguring well. This is why we stayed in Madina forty days."

When the Imām and his party returned to Makka they found that most of the pilgrims had departed and quiet had succeeded the bustling activity of the season. These days were recalled by the Imām later on in Hadramawt thus: "The year we went to *ḥajj* we saw in Makka, during the season, much *madad* and openings. When we returned to it from Madina we found it more vacant. Presence [of the heart] and awe were more during the season, but afterwards it was more leisurely. These (presence and awe) should be sought toward the end of the night, when a third or a quarter of the night remains and there are around the house no more that one or two persons. This is when presence and awe occur, for when the Divine Unveiling (*tajallī*) occurs it is distributed amongst those who are there. The less people there are the more the share of each one is, and the more there are the less [their shares]…."

There were repeated requests from the people of the two sanctuaries to remain with them. He said, "Makka is good for [only] one of three: a man totally obscure whom nobody knows and who is like the dust. That is, he cares nothing if trodden upon. A wanderer in the mountains as was Shaykh Ibn al-Fāriḍ, or an ocean who is neither per-

The Sanctuary of the Kaᶜba in Makka a century ago.

turbed nor oppressed by the crowd that gathers around him, who is not distracted by them from God, and on condition that he is well steeped in the Book and *sunna* and their practical application. Such a man may remain in the two sanctuaries, take of the goodness they offer and remain safe from their perils. As for a man of lesser stature, they will preoccupy and weary him with wordly things and situations."

Another great ᶜAlawī, Sayyid Muḥammad Sheliye sent Imām al Ḥaddād a verbal message, instructing the messenger thus: "Tell him he is sending you his *salām* and advising you not to stay." The messenger, who knew the Imām told the *sayyid*, "He has no intention of doing so." "Tell him nevertheless," replied Sayyid Sheliye. The Imām answered him saying, "Staying is not on my mind. We had never intended it to begin with because of what we saw of the behavior of the people of the two sanctuaries." Imām al-Ḥaddād had never been inclined to allow infringements to go undenounced, and in the sacred land he was even less disposed to do so. He told the people of the Hijāz, "Were we to stay with you we would complain about you to the ruler because of what we observe of your condition." And he advised the people to think well of the people of the Hijāz, and in order to be able to do so and maintain courtesy he told them, "In the two sanctuaries look at nothing except the Sacred House and the Blessed Chamber; look at nothing else."

It is evidently impossible to know what spiritual experiences the Imām went through during his *ḥajj* voyage. The very word 'experience' is afterall already inadequate for things of that order. Apart from his uncle's prediction that light shall be poured upon him without intermediary, however, there are mysterious indications in a letter which he wrote to Shaykh Ḥusayn Bā-Faḍl after his return to

Hadramawt. Shaykh Bā-Faḍl must have been himself a gnostic of the highest order, since the letter was couched in terms that could only be understood by such masters. Here is a short passage of that letter: "Pray for us," the Imām writes, "that we may return to these locations upon which dawn the lights of the special [Divine] Manifestation, for this is what we yearn and thirst for and our visit has only increased our thirst and longing. The sight [of these places] has aroused in the heart something that had been dormant therein, and which has since persisted in a manner that had not been there before. The comfort and repose that had existed before the meeting have been transformed into a longing that worries and unsettles the heart; beneath these words lies the secret of the meaning of the manifestation of the Real in the bush and the dawning of that light on the "Mount of the Summons."[60] You are one to understand the allusion to that which is inexpressible."

Shaykh Bā-Faḍl had already spoken to the Imām thus: "I had two seas from which to scoop, a sea of outward knowledge (Shaykh Aḥmad al-Qushāshī) and a sea of inward knowledge (Sayyid Muḥammad ibn ᶜAlawī al-Saqqāf.) Now God has united the two seas in you." To others he used to say, "I have met with three men, one whose spiritual state outstripped his words, that was Sayyid Muḥammad ibn ᶜAlawī, another whose words outstripped his state, that was Shaykh Aḥmad al-Qushāshī, and another who was perfect in both his state and his speech, my master Imām ᶜAbdallāh al-Ḥaddād." He is also reported to have said, "I went on *ḥajj* many times, but I count only the occasion when I was in the company of my master ᶜAbdallāh, for I have strong hopes that this one shall be accepted and that I shall obtain that which I desire."

Imām ᶜAbdallāh al-Ḥaddād never had the opportunity to return to the Hijāz as had been his desire and many of the poems he composed in the following years and until his death were full of yearning for those places.

Chapter 14
SUPERNATURAL EVENTS

What is a karāma? The Imām's view on such happenings—examples of supernatural events.

Miraculous events are frequent occurrences in the lives of Divine Messengers and saints. These events are primary phenomena in the case of Divine Messengers, the purpose of which is to prove the truth of their mission, challenge their opponents, and strengthen the faith of their followers. For saints, they are secondary phenomena related to the perfection of their following in the footsteps of their Prophet or Divine Messenger, and are part of what they receive as his spiritual heirs or deputies. This is why Muslim scholars make a clear distinction between the miracles of the Prophets, which they call *muʿjiza,* and those of the saints, which they call *karāma*. The *karāma* of the *walī* is considered a *muʿjiza* of his Prophet, since it is only through the *baraka* of the latter that it is possible. "A *muʿjiza,*" said the Imām, "is proof of the Messenger's veracity, whereas a *karāma* from a *walī* who firmly upholds the law is proof of the excellence of his following of his Prophet and of the truth of his religion."

The first to show such supernatural feats after the Prophet were his Companions, and then the generation that followed them. Numerous other such occurrences were recorded in history, and the pattern continues unbroken to the present day. As the times degenerate, however, and the hearts of people become more and more engrossed in material pursuits and correspondingly less open to spirituality, the frequency of these occurrences diminishes and those capable of producing them become much more careful to hide them from the eyes of ordinary men. The reasons for this are twofold. First, some of these phenomena may be produced by means other than the spiritual power of the *walī,* means which are in effect their exact opposite, that is, means by which the energies of the lower worlds are brought into play. Second, the state of today's people makes them more inclined to deny, oppose, and antagonize the elect. Some deny the possibility of sanctification as such, others concede it but only for those long dead, others still acknowledge it in general but invariably deny it to any particular *shaykh*. The *walī* therefore hides his election aspects to avoid pushing such people, perhaps driven by jealousy and resentment, into a position of antagonism. This may lead them down an extremely perilous road, not because the *walī* is likely to retaliate—for such people are by definition the most forbearant and forgiving—but because God says in His *ḥadith qudsī*, "Those who antagonize a *walī* of Mine, upon them I declare war." The worst thing that may happen to those upon whom God declares war is for them to lose their faith and die as disbelievers. This is one reason why, when a man once came to Imām al-Ḥaddād to inform him that he had committed to writing a number of the Imām's *karāmāt*, he was sharply rebuked and ordered to dissolve it in water. It was only near the very end of his life that he gave his disciples permission to recount what they had seen or heard, and it was only after his death that his main biographer, Sayyid Muḥammad ibn Zayn ibn Sumayṭ, collected from those who had known him as many of these stories as he could to include in his biography. The number of stories he collected reached two hundred and eighty six, these being the events that were remembered by the disciples who survived the Imām. Much was lost with those who died before him. Sayyid Ḥasan al-Jufrī, who had known the Imām in his younger days, used to say, "Had I wished to record twenty *karāmāt* for the *sayyid* each day, I would have done so." The Imām, as do other men of God, often spoke disparagingly of their *karāmāt,* indicating thereby that these constituted no proof of their nearness to God and furthermore were a dangerous source of pride and ostentation for the unaccomplished saint. They were also likely to distract the disciples from the real goal of the path which is the knowledge of the Eternal and Immutable, not that of the changeful and contingent. A seeker who struggles for the purpose of obtaining supernatural powers is one who has been blinded by created phenomena and arrested in his path to the Creator. The Imām once said that to wish for such things was good only for children and yarn spinners, meaning old women. On another occasion he said; "Supernatural events are within easy reach of God's generosity and power, for those He honors. They are also within the power of devils, however. The important thing is rectitude. If someone is said to be able to fly in the air, so does the devil fly from the East to the West in an instant. This is not done by saints except when strictly necessary."

The supernatural events that travelers are discouraged to aim or yearn for are outward physical phenomena. As the Imām said, "This applies to those who seek outward *karāmāt* such as the folding up of distances, speaking of hidden things, and so on. As for those who seek real *karāmāt* such as an increase in faith and certitude, realizing the relinquishment of all desire for the world, aspiring for the hereafter, and other such things, these are praiseworthy, for they are part of religion and the truth which should be aspired for and pursued." It is worthy of note that the Imām calls inward realization the "real" *karāma*, implying that outward phenomena are illusory *karāmāt*.

The explanation of supernatural events lies in the power of the spirit, when unleashed by the neutralization of the body's appetites and the soul's deviant tendencies, which constitute the downward pulling tendency. The relationship between the spirit and the body is then reversed; the spirit gains near total supremacy, and the body becomes as it were spiritualized, thus escaping from the limitations of density, gravity, time, and distance. Such a person is able to bring into play the forces of the higher worlds and use his spiritual power to extend his sensory and motor powers far beyond what the common man is capable of imagining. He is also able to perceive and intervene in other worlds such as the *Barzakh*, the world of the jinn, and the seven heavens, as well as see into the past and the future. This is how Imām al-Ḥaddād was capable of walking on his own during his childhood, and of going from his retreat at al-Hujāyra mosque to the cemetery without the help of a guide or a staff, keeping to the middle of the street and returning by another route. When one of his disciples asked him how he could have authored so many books despite his blindness, he replied simply by remarking, "There is a fly in your coffee." He also used to say, before leading the prayer, "Straighten your ranks, for I can see you behind me!"

Two men once arrived from ᶜĪnāt to Tarīm. One of them expressed his wish to visit the Imām, but the other tried to convince him otherwise. They parted company and the first, hoping that the Imām would come out for the *Ẓuhr* prayer, arrived before midday only to be told that the Imām had not come out at that time for a year now because of the weakness that had overtaken him in his last years. This meant that the visitor had to remain there until the *ᶜAṣr* prayer and this worried him, for he was thus liable to miss the company he was due to travel back with. A few moments later the Imām appeared and the congregation in the mosque, understanding that the visitor was responsible for this unusual event, promptly congratulated him saying, "It is only your intention that has brought him out." He rose to the Imām, kissed his hand, and was asked, "What did that man say to you? Tell him if you do not come to us we shall come to you." He then placed his palm on his chest, reciting something, then when he was done, exhorted him to remain in God's obedience.

He was also capable of communicating with animals. Once, as he entered the mosque of al-Hujayra accompanied by one of his disciples, the latter noticed a chameleon standing at the door. As they were sitting down the Imām said, "Go tell the chameleon that his request has been granted." The disciple rose to his feet and carried out the Imām's instructions, following which the chameleon swiftly departed. Surprised, he returned to the Imām asking for an explanation. The Imām said, "He complained about certain jinn and we have arranged things for him."

Again, once in his latter years, when he had become extremely hard of hearing, he spent the night in a certain valley. In the morning he asked his companions, "Do you expect rain today?" They replied, "No, Sayyidī, none of us has observed lightning nor heard thunder." He said, "It may yet come, for when I rose for my night prayer, I heard what sounded like thunder." No sooner had he spoken than the rain started falling.

When a disciple came to his house intending to consult him about his intention to marry a certain woman, the

Imām's servant came to the door saying, "Sayyidī says: if you wish to consult him, don't, unless you intend to comply with whatever he tells you." This gave the disciple the certainty than the Imām already knew everything he had wanted to tell him; consequently when he advised him not to marry her, he obeyed.

Many men became his disciples through dream visions and many more experienced his ability to succor spatially remote people in perilous situations. A certain ᶜUmar ibn ᶜAbdallāh recounts his own experience thus: "The cause of my attachment to the *shaykh* is that I was praying in a mosque in Shibām, then fell asleep and saw the Prophet, may God's blessings and peace be upon him. Each person asked him a question and received an answer. He came toward me saying, 'And you, what do you ask?' I said: 'What makes a *shaykh*?' He immediately replied, 'Knowledge.' Four days later, in another dream vision, I saw a man walk up and down in the same mosque. Whenever he approached me he looked me straight in the face repeating this thrice. This man captured my heart entirely. When I woke up I made inquiries and was told this description was that of Sayyid ᶜAbdallāh. I took a journey to him and, as I set eyes on him, recognized him for the man in the dream. Then I remained near him until his death." This man also recounted how, when rain was pouring down in Shibām and the area was flooded, he and two other men attempted to cross a stream but the torrential force of the water overcame them and threatened to drown them. He screamed, repeatedly calling the Imām for help, and soon heard a voice calling back, "Over here, I am your companion." He followed the voice thinking it was one of his companions and soon found himself on high ground. One of his companions was carried away by the water and drowned. He had a few days rest and then headed for Tarīm to see the Imām. He said nothing once he reached the Imām's house. A few days later a man spoke of him to the Imām, asking him to look after him. He was told, "We have taken care of him in the torrent, are we to do otherwise in other situations?" Only then did ᶜUmar know whose voice it was that saved him.

A man by the name of Sālim sought the Imām's advice regarding a journey he wished to undertake. The Imām told him to go to *ḥajj* instead, adding, "We shall be with you and keep our gaze on you." Sālim was pleased and complied. As he was at sea, off the coast of Northern Yemen, the ship was caught in a storm and, seeing themselves about to drown, everyone panicked. Sālim called as loudly as he could: "Yā Sayyidī ᶜAbdallāh, Yā Ḥaddād!" repeating the call ceaselessly. Then, remembering how the Imām had told him that he would be with him, he reproached him for having abandoned him. Soon the sea regained its calm and he pursued his voyage peaceably and completed his *ḥajj*. When he returned he went to see the Imām who, as soon as he took his hand, before he could say anything, said, "O Sālim, you have treated us unjustly when you said such and such a thing," repeating word for word the reproaches Sālim had uttered and had by then forgotten.

Another of the Imām's companions recounted how he suffered from an eye ailment for two weeks. When at the height of his pains he went to the Imām, kissed his foot and begged for help, he touched his eye and his head, recited some Qur'ān, and before long the pain had vanished. Another man said that he was struck with a sickness in his hand which caused him tremendous pain. In his sleep he saw the Imām stroking his hand. He woke up to find that there were no longer any trace of pain. Yet another man who was moribund, his family expecting his imminent death, saw in a dream vision a man on a mare, who took him behind him, then galloped until they reached the tomb of Shaykh Saᶜīd ibn ᶜĪsā al-ᶜAmūdī. The *shaykh* came out from his tomb to meet them and the rider requested from him to intercede for an extension of the sick man's life. Shaykh Saᶜīd handed him a letter that he placed in his turban, while remounting. He took the patient behind him, and galloped back to their starting point. The patient recovered rapidly, then, some time later, went to visit the Imām, whom he had never seen before. He immediately recognized him for the man in the dream, and the mare before the house as the one that carried them both to and from Qaydūn, Shaykh al ᶜAmūdī's town.

There are countless other such stories, a small number of which took place after the Imām's death. One of his companions suffered a severe pain in his eye which persisted until, in his own words, he wished that his eye would come out altogether, that the pain be relieved. Then he received news of the Imām's death, hesitated a little, then decided to attend the funeral prayer come what may. The pain persisted throughout the funeral, however, to his surprise, it disappeared completely before he had had time to reach home. There was no doubt in his mind that this was the *baraka* of the Imām.

Chapter 15
THE LAST DAYS

The Imām's prediction of the time of his own death—the first signs of illness—receiving visitors during his terminal illness—investiture of his disciple al-Shajjār—death of the Imām—the funeral—supernatural events following his death.

A great many years before his death, on one of his visits to the cemetery, the Imām came out of the mausoleum of Imām al-ᶜAydarūs, walked to the exact spot where he was later to be buried, and stood there for a while saying, "*My Lord! Cause me to land at a blessed landing place, for you are the best to cause to land.*" [23:29] More than once he had hinted that his death was to follow that of his lifetime friend, Sayyid ᶜAlī al-ᶜAydarūs. After the latter's passing away, he replied to a man who was saying to him, "May God prolong your life!" by saying, "There is no further prolongation, Sayyid ᶜAlī ibn ᶜAbdallāh is waiting for me." Again, when one of his companions came to consult him about going on *ḥajj*, instead of encouraging him to do so as had always been his custom, he said, "If you wish you may go, or if you wish you may attend." The man did not understand at that time what the word "attend" meant. He therefore decided to go and returned to take leave saying, "May God not make this my last meeting with you!" To which the reply was: "How long [do you think] my life [is to be prolonged?] There is no more living after eighty eight years and the matter is neither yours nor mine [to decide], but God's, August and Majestic be He!"

The Imām remained in good health, regularly attending the five prayers, the sessions of teaching and remembrance, and the *tarawīḥ* prayers, until Thursday the 27th of Ramaḍān 1132 H. when the first signs that all was not well appeared. On that day he came out neither for the ᶜ*Aṣr* prayer, nor the following reading session. Nevertheless, he instructed his disciples to read as was their custom. He complained that the pain that he had occasionally suffered from had gripped him more severely. He still came out for the ᶜ*Ishā'* prayer and stayed through the *tarawīḥ,* but failed to attend the Friday prayer the next day. This indicated, in no uncertain way, that something was seriously wrong. He was also unable to attend the completion of the Qur'ān on the eve of the 29th, and the ᶜ*Ishā'* prayer on the eve of the ᶜ*Īd.* On ᶜ*Īd* day he was visited by Sayyid Zayn al-ᶜAbedīn and his brother. They arrived at midmorning and sat with him for a long time. He told them that he thought his illness was due to his lack of courtesy, and explained it by saying that he had visited his wife from the house of Faqīh on the eve of the 26th, to please and comfort her, knowing fully well that the Prophet, may God's blessings and peace be upon him, forsook all worldly affairs during the last ten days and nights of the month, including his wives, and remained in retreat in the mosque. He then complained of pain in the loins saying that this was what had prevented him from attending the prayers. Among other things he said, "One should not impose upon the body the dictates of one's resolution (*himma*). It has been said that the resolution of the intelligent man is more powerful than his body, while the body of the ignorant man is more powerful than his resolution." He also recounted to them the dream where he had seen himself and Sayyid ᶜAlī ibn ᶜAbdallāh and understood from this that he was shortly to follow him to the other world. He also mentioned many of the *sayyids* who had reached ages above ninety, thereby indicating the proximity of his own death. At this point, he no longer permitted anyone else to visit him until the 3rd of Shawwāl. To the elderly *sayyids* who then came in and greeted him, he mentioned that they should pray for him and added, "God's doing is nothing but beneficence and justice. What comes to the servant from God comes according to God's will, not the servant's own wishes."

Five days later he again allowed for visitors, although he was initially uninclined because they were too numerous. He remained reclining on his bed. A poem was recited, then the *Fātiḥa,* then he said, "Tell them [to take leave] with their hearts," meaning that they were not to take his hand. Then, on subsequent days, he sent someone to the door to tell the awaiting visitors: "Leave me to my Lord, do not impose upon me to excess. I remember you and I pray for you, so pray for me."

On the 16th he sent for al-Sḥajjār who arrived to find only Sayyid Ḥasan at his father's bedside. The Imām reminded his son of a tunic he had worn for a while then folded up and kept aside. "We want it for *al-Ḥāj,"* he said, "allow no one else to take it, otherwise he would miss that which is of account, the visible and the invisible investiture." When the shirt was brought he unfolded it, held it to his chest, made as if he was about to wear it, then he refolded it, blew of his breath and spittle onto it, uttered the *dhikr* of God and the prayer upon His Messenger, then gave it to al-Sḥajjār saying, "Here! We have invested you now and authorize you to invest whomsoever you should wish who qualifies for it. We have already invested you [with the *khirqa*] many times before and we hope that you will receive it again, we also hope that God will grant you the real investiture and cause you to qualify for it, too."

On the 18th he sent someone out with this message: "I will not force myself to sit up for you, and I have no wish to receive you lying down. Pray for me and I shall pray for you."

During the course of his illness one of his sons asked him what name he should give the child that his wife was about to deliver. The Imām told him to call him ᶜAbdallāh. The custom of the land was that no newborn was to be named after his grandfather until after the latter's death.

The 19th was a Friday. As the people waited outside, there arrived Sayyid Zayn al-ᶜAbedīn and they were permitted to enter in his company. He asked the Imām how he had slept and he answered, "More than when I was in good health." Then the Imām called al-Sḥajjār, "Aḥmad!" He immediately answered, "*labbayk!*" He was somewhat surprised, since it was the first time in the seventeen years that he had known him that he had called him by his name, his usual form of address having been *al-Ḥāj*. The Imām asked him to pray for him and he replied that he had just done so at the grave of al-Faqīh al-Muqaddam. "Yes!" said the Imām. "Make *duᶜā'* there!"

The next day there appeared a swelling the size of an egg below the navel.

Then Shaykh ᶜUmar al-ᶜAmūdī arrived together with about ten of his companions. It had not been his custom to visit the Imām at such a time, but he may have sensed the urgency of the situation. He waited for two days before being granted permission to enter. He kissed the Imām's hand. "Welcome to the ᶜAmūdī, welcome to the ᶜAmūdī, welcome to the ᶜAmūdī," the Imām greeted him. Then, seeing his desire to rub his face against him, he said, " Rub. Let him rub!" Then he recited the *Fātiḥa*, raised his hands and prayed for them, and then they departed.

One of the household women saw in her sleep that she was speaking with another woman. Then she saw a man climb up to the roof and she asked the other woman, "Who is this?"The reply was: "This is 'Delight,' he has come up to his beloved." The dream was recounted to the Imām who was pleased with it.

In the last six days of his life his movements became heavy and he remained deeply absorbed for long periods. He often raised his hands then clasped them across his chest as though in prayer. He then moved them down to his knees, raising up the right index finger as would a man reciting the *tashahhud.*

On the 2nd of Dhul-Qa^cda, al-Sḥajjār entered his room and saw him lying on his bed, so thin that there was hardly any flesh covering his bones. Twenty years before he had told his son that his wish was that on the day he died there would remain on him no flesh at all, and that he also wished that his terminal illness would be brief. This last remark arose from his wish not to impose the difficulties of a long illness on those around him, despite the fact that many a great man of God, and he made especial mention of Sayyid Aḥmad al-Rifā^cī, had desired a long illness. But as he said, "Where would you find those who would patiently endure your illness should it be prolonged? Were someone to assist in your *wuḍū'* two or three times he would find you tiresome and disagreeable." This he said despite the utter selfless devotion shown by his son al-Ḥasan who had the privilege of serving him during the forty days between the onset of his illness and his death. He was the one who later recounted how the Imām in his last days kept repeating the last *ḥadith* in the book of Imām al-Bukhārī, "There are two words which are light to utter, heavy in the scales, and dear to the All-Merciful: *Subḥān Allahī wa biḥamdihi, subḥān Allāhil-ᶜAẓīm.*"

The swelling subsided a few days later but his voice first became hoarse, then very weak. From then on his only sustenance was curdled milk, two or three cups a day. He asked them to sprinkle water over him and they thought he felt feverish. When they offered him water to drink to help with the fever, however, he refused, which left them somewhat perplexed. Al-Shajjār points out in his book that both the hoarseness in his voice and the request for water to be sprinkled were further evidence of his identification with the Prophet, may God's blessings and peace be upon him, for both these had occurred during his final illness in Madina.

On the eve of the 8th of Dhul-Qaᶜda of the year 1132, at the age of eighty eight lunar years, and when the first quarter of the night had gone by, the Imām breathed his last in his house at al-Ḥāwī, and his son Sayyid al-Ḥasan saw a flash of light shooting out from the body.

They kept the news from the household and the resident disciples until after the dawn prayer, when Sayyid ᶜAlawī, the eldest son who had just led the prayer, bid the man usually responsible for reciting the *Fātiḥas,* "Recite the *Fātiḥa* for your *ḥabīb!*" There was a great commotion the moment he had said this and the congregation was unable to complete the *Fātiḥa* or proceed with the usual invocations that followed the prayer. Messengers were sent with the news to the neighboring towns and to the mosques so that the *Fātiḥa* would be offered to the Imām following the ritual prayer, this being the custom of the land to convey the news so that those who wished to attend the funeral might be enabled to do so. Soon the house was packed with people. They filled the mosque, the corridors, the staircase, the roof, the yard, and the whole surrounding area including the palm tree plantation.

On that morning, in Makka, one of those employed to sweep the sanctuary informed the people that the Imām had died. He was evidently a man of God, and when asked how he knew this, he answered that he usually saw him every day and every night circumambulate the Ka[c]ba, but that the night before he had not seen him and had thus deduced that he had died.

The ritual washing was performed by Sayyid al-Ḥasan with the help of another *sayyid*. The water ran down the spout into the external gutter and was received by the people in all sorts of vessels for its *baraka*; not one drop was allowed to reach the ground. He was then shrouded in a cloth offered to him by Sayyid [c]Alī ibn [c]Abdallāh, which he had kept for this purpose. After the *[c]Aṣr* prayer the bier was carried on the heads and shoulders of men. There was much jostling and shoving, each eager to have his share. They reached the cemetery shortly before sunset and the burial was completed after night had fallen. The crowd spread as far as the eye could see in all directions. Once the burial was over an Indian dervish appeared and throwing himself down on the grave, cried out and rubbed his face in the dust. They forced him to move aside. Then the Imām's great tent was erected over the grave, the same tent he used on his visits to theProphet Hūd, may peace be upon him. Under its shade sat those who would recite the Qur'ān for the usual three days. They read the whole day and about one quarter of the night, then they recited some invocations and departed, leaving al-Sḥajjār and the other disciples to carry on for a while longer and then rest around the grave till before dawn. There was hardly a moment, day or night,

The tombstone of the grave of the Imām
with his lineage engraved on it.

The grave of the Imām and the graves of his wives and children.

when people who had not attended the funeral arrived, prayed the funeral prayer before the grave, made *du'a'* for themselves and the Imām, and then went away carrying some of the dust overlying the grave. They carried away so much that, after being initially elevated, it came down almost to ground level. The recitation of the Qur'ān was completed on Friday the 11th. More people attended the ceremony than those present at the burial. The Imām's sons arranged ample catering for those who came.

A *sayyid* then saw in his sleep that the Imām was holding small folded pieces of paper in his hand and was distributing them to those who had attended his funeral. On being given one, this *sayyid* opened it and found it blank. This was interpreted as the erasure of sins and the covering up of blemishes.

At a later date, when al-Shajjār left Hadramawt he was told at Aden, al-Hudayyida, and every other Yemeni port where he stopped that news of the Imām's death had been brought to them by a dervish. He was unable to ascertain whether it was the same man they had seen at the funeral.

Another of the Imām's companions, a man by the name of ᶜAlī Hurmuz later said, "I met a dervish who looked Turkish near the seaside at al-Hudayyida and he spoke to me and said, 'My condolences for Sayyid ᶜAbdallāh al-Ḥaddād.' I was stunned and asked him, 'Has he died?' He replied, 'Yes. And I was there and have prayed on him. It is not yet three days since he died.'"

There were scores of dream visions relating to this event and the poems and eulogies ran into hundreds.

There were many people who regretted having missed the benefits of the Imām's company during his lifetime. Years before, he had said, "They shall not know our worth until we leave them. As long as a man remains among them they do not know his worth, but when he becomes a tomb, then they know his worth." And when it was reported to him that someone had said, "There is [nothing] in Tarīm save al-Faqīh al-Muqaddam in the cemetery and Sayyid ᶜAbdallāh al-Ḥaddād among the living," he said, "And truly superior is al-Faqīh al-Muqaddam. But he is now a tomb, while the one who is here is the gate, and a gate is not the same as a tomb. They will not recognize the gate until he leaves them and becomes a tomb, and things will happen to them about which they will say, 'This was the gate from whence things came to us.'" Al-Shajjār explained in a short commentary that the first mentioned "things" are of the kinds which injure and vex, while the second mentioned are of those which comfort and delight.

Many years after the Imām's death one of his grandsons, Sayyid Aḥmad ibn al-Ḥasan, read whilst in Makka that Shaykh ᶜAlī Wafā, the great gnostic *shaykh* from Egypt had said that he saw the Prophets and saints arriving at the Kaᶜba during the second half of certain nights of the week. He decided to attempt to see his grandfather and on one such night entered the sanctuary. Having completed his circumambulation, he stood at the *multazam* loudly making *duᶜā'*. He felt someone's hand on his back and a voice said, "Pray silently!" He turned around and recognized his grandfather by the descriptions he had frequently heard of him at home. The Imām raised his hands and prayed silently while his grandson stood on his right, hands raised, saying, "*Āmīn*," to the *duᶜā'* he could not hear. When the Imām had finished he rubbed his face with his hands and headed toward the Syrian corner of the Kaᶜba. Sayyid Aḥmad began to follow, intending to speak to him, but suddenly he was nowhere to be found, despite the fact that at that time of the night there were only two other people within the precinct.

Chapter 16
THE SUCCESSION

The Imām's son al-Ḥasan and grandson Aḥmad—Ḥabīb Ṭāhir ibn ᶜUmar al-Ḥaddād and his descendants—Ḥabīb Aḥmad Mashhūr al-Ḥaddād—successors from other Bā-ᶜAlawī clans.

Imām ᶜAbdallāh al-Ḥaddād had six sons, all of whom were saints of considerable stature. To succeed him as the head of the al-Ḥaddād family, however, the choice fell on his fourth son al-Ḥasan, supported to a certain extent by his elder brother, ᶜAlawī. Al-Ḥasan became a major scholar, an Imām in his own right. He was awe inspiring and very strictly conformed to his father's method, bringing up his children and grandchildren to follow the same pattern. He died in 1188 H. and was succeeded by his son Aḥmad, again an Imām of immense erudition. His spiritual resolution was such that when his ship struck a rock in the Red Sea and sank, he remained hanging onto a wooden plank for five days and never missed a ritual prayer, replacing the prescribed movements with nods of the head. When a boat arrived to rescue the survivors, he insisted on being the last to be pulled out of the sea. He was succeeded at his death in 1204 H. by his son ᶜUmar followed by another of his sons, ᶜAlawī, who followed in the footsteps of his forefathers and authored over a hundred books.

Major figures also appeared in the progeny of Sayyid ᶜAlawī son of Imām ᶜAbdallāh. Among the most illustrious were *Ḥabīb* Ṭāhir ibn ᶜUmar who lived and died in the town of Qaydūn and his son Muḥammad ibn Ṭāhir whose spiritual state was so intense that he died a few years before his father on one of his trips to Indonesia at the age of forty two. His two sons ᶜAlawī and Ḥusayn, both great gnostic *shaykhs*, lived in Indonesia. The first was a scholar and public figure, but the second preferred to remain in relative obscurity.

Of the descendants of *sayyid* ᶜUmar, Imām ᶜAbdallāh's younger brother, mention must be made of the two brothers ᶜAbdallāh and ᶜAlawī, sons of Ṭāhir al-Ḥaddād. They were major scholars, recognized by scholars and laymen alike and accorded great respect since in their early twenties. They founded the *ribāṭ* or religious school of Qaydūn. *Ḥabīb* ᶜAlawī was later to move to Malaya, where he became Mufti of the sultanate of Johore until his death in 1382 H. The foremost student produced by the *ribāṭ* of Qaydūn was undoubtedly *Ḥabīb* Aḥmad Mashhūr al-Ḥaddād. He received intensive attention from *Ḥabīb* ᶜAbdallāh and *Ḥabīb* ᶜAlawī, as well as from all other major ᶜAlawī figures of his time—and a great many they were. His first trip to Africa, at the age of twenty-two, took him to Zanzibar. The people of the Island crowded into the mosque to see the young *sayyid* of whom everyone was already speaking. It was Ramaḍān; he sat teaching and explaining the Qur'ān. It took him two weeks to discourse on a single verse of the *Fātiḥa*. Four years later he returned to East Africa, this time to the port of Mombasa in Kenya where he was eventually to settle. Every year, whether from Hadramawt or from Kenya, he went to *Ḥajj*. He ceaselessly moved from one village to another in Kenya, inviting people to Islam, educating the Muslims, and propagating the easy spiritual method of Imām al-Ḥaddād. In 1375 H. (1956 C.E.), he moved to Kampala, Uganda, where he remained for about thirteen years. In

Masjid al-Fatḥ, the Imām's mosque at al-Ḥāwī after its recent renovation.

Interior of Masjid al-Fatḥ after renovation.

Uganda alone an estimated sixty thousand Africans accepted Islam at his hands. Many more accepted Islam in Kenya. Under his guidance mosques were erected, Islamic schools founded, teaching sessions established, and important religious occasions celebrated.

His book, *Key to the Garden*, originally written in Arabic during his sojourn in Uganda, has been translated into English and other languages. It is a masterly exposition of the doctrine of Divine Unity, the first and most important pillar of Islam, in its three dimensions of *Islām, Īmān*, and *Iḥsān*, or *sharī^{c}a*, *ṭarīqa*, and *haqīqa*. His poems have been collected into a *Dīwān*, which he was most reluctant to publish. His sons and grandsons were educated by him in the purest ^{c}Alawī tradition. He remained one of the foremost leaders of the ^{c}Alawīs until his death in Jeddah on the 14th of Rajab 1416 H. (6th December 1995).

We have mentioned here only a few of the important figure of al-Ḥaddād descent. The number of great men in this family easily runs into dozens, however, the purpose of this work was only to show that the tradition remains strong and effective, the unbroken chain of masters extending down from Imām al-Ḥaddād to this day being the guarantee of its orthodoxy and vitality, as well as its being the continuation of that extension up from the Imām to the Prophet, may God's blessings and peace be upon him and his family.

The method of the Imām was propagated, not only by his descendants, but also by his disciples, most of whom were of ^{c}Alawī lineage, such as Imām Aḥmad ibn Zayn al-Ḥabashī, Imām ^{c}Abdal-Raḥmān Bīlfaqīh, Imām ^{c}Umar ibn ^{c}Abdal-Raḥmān al-Bār, the two ibn Sumayṭ brothers, and a few non-^{c}Alawīs, the best known of whom being Shaykh Aḥmad al-Shajjār. Near the end of his life the Imām said to al-Shajjār, "You now have the authority to accept disciples, but only in my name not in yours." This meant that he could receive disciples into the path and transmit the spiritual influence that he himself had received from the Imām, authorize them to recite the various *awrād*, and supervise their progress, but only so long as he did so as the Imām's deputy, not as an independent *shaykh*. It was understood that this was to take place after the Imām's death, since al-Sḥajjār had no intention of returning to his country before that. The Imām also authorized him to dispense the *khirqa*, again in his name. In effect, once back in his country, al-Sḥajjār seems to have enjoyed almost total autonomy and to have had many disciples, at least one of whom, a man from Madina, became well known as a scholar and Sufi.

As for the Imām's direct descendants, they followed the pattern laid down centuries before by Imām Abū Bakr ibn ᶜAbdallāh al-ᶜAydarūs, who despite having himself reached the supreme station, still dispensed the *khirqa* and gave the *ijāza* in his father's name. This indicates that he still considered his father, Imām ᶜAbdallāh al-ᶜAydarūs, to be the effective head of the order, while he himself acted only as his deputy. Thus do the masters of the house of al-Ḥaddād still say to their disciples that their *shaykh* is Imām al-Ḥaddād and that their own function is merely to link them to him. Those attached to Imām al-Ḥaddād do indeed experience his presence whenever needed. A *sayyid* from Madina once told me how, when he was greatly perplexed by the concept of wordless speech used by theologians to describe Divine speech, he saw Imām al-Ḥaddād in a dream-vision holding him to his chest and conversing with him at length without a word being exchanged between them. Thoughts were transmitted and understood prior to their verbal formulation. This is one instance of how the Imām clarified a difficult matter for his disciple. However, it is well known among Sufis that only under very exceptional circumstances would the disciple be able to progress without being under the authority and supervision of a living master, still dwelling in body on earth. This is why those following the al-Ḥaddād path must first of all attach themselves firmly to one of the living masters of the method, then through him to the Imām.

Notes

1. Al-Ḥākim, *al-Mustadrak* 3312, Ṭabarānī, *al-Muᶜjam al-Kabīr, 3/46; al-Awsaṭ,* 3/283, 6/251, 6/406; *al-Ṣaghīr*, 1/139, 2/22; al-Bazzār, *Kashf al-Astār,* 3/222; Abū Nuᶜaym, *Ḥilyat'al-Awliyā',* 4/306.

2. Muslim, *Kitāb Faḍā'il al-Ṣaḥāba, Bāb min faḍā'il ᶜAlī ibn Abī Ṭālib,* 36,37; Tirmidhī, *Kitāb al-Manāqib*, 31; Dārimī, *Faḍā'il al-Qur'ān*, 1; Aḥmad, 3:14, 17, 26.

3. Quoted by the late Sayyid Muḥammad al-Shātirī in his book on the names of the various ᶜAlawī clans: *Al-Muᶜjam al-Laṭīf*, published by *ᶜĀlam al-Maᶜrifa*, Jeddah, 1989, pp. 81, 82.

4. We use the term Gnostic as equivalent to the Arabic *ᶜĀrif*, knower.Gnosis is direct spiritual knowledge of Divine realities. A Gnostic is he who is given to witness these realities.

5. We must stress the fact that these masters were meticulous followers of *sharīᶜa* and never expected such words to be taken to mean that religious obligations such as ritual prayers, fasts, *zakāt*, and so on could be neglected and replaced by sitting with a saint. On the contrary, never are these obligations carried out with more sincerity and precision than by those who keep the company of saints and emulate their behavior.

6. Laṭā'if al-Minan: Famous work by the Shādhilī shaykh ibn ᶜAṭā'illāh, devoted to the life, spiritual states, and teachings of his shaykh, Abul-ᶜAbbās al-Mursī and the latter's master Abul-Ḥasan al-Shādhilī, the founder of the order. An English translation of this work is to appear in 2005, Fons Vitae, as *The Subtle Blessings*, translated by N. Roberts.

7. Al-Hikam: This collection of sufi aphorisms by Shaykh ibn ᶜAṭā'illāh became one the most widely read works on Sufism and is still used in teaching circles by Sufi shaykhs all over the world.

8. Ibn Kathīr, *Tafsīr,* 3/439.

9. Tirmidhī, *Kitāb Thawāb al-Qur'ān*, 9.

10. The World of the Command, *ᶜālam al-amr*, is the spiritual world beyond all formal creation.

11. Only one *Jumuᶜa* is held in Tarīm in the Grand Mosque. According to Imām Shafiᶜī, if the mosque is capable of accommodating everyone it is not permissible to hold another *Jumuᶜa* elsewhere.

12. *Red Sulphur or the Supreme Elixir*, by Imām cAbdallāh ibn Abū Bakr al-cAydarūs Bā-cAlawī, Cairo, 1352 A.H, 1933 C.E.

13. Tirmidhī, *Kitāb al-Manāqib*, 31.

14. Bukhārī, *Kitāb al-Īmān*, 8.

15. Bayhaqī, *Shucab al-Īmān,* 2/189.

16. Bukharī, *Kitāb al-Riqāq*, 38.

17. Tirmidhī, *Kitāb al-Zuhd*, 57.

18. *Allāhū lā ilāhā illā Huwa'l' Ḥayyu'l' Qayyūm,* [*Yā Qawiy* 30 times] *lā ta'khudhuhu sinatun walā nawm, lahu māfis' samāwāti wa mā fil' arḍ,* [*Yā Qawiy* 30 times] *man dhā' lladhī yashfacu cindahu illā bi idhnih, yaclamu mā bayna aydīhim wa mā khalfahum walā yuḥiṭūna bishay'in min cilmihi illā bimā shā',* [*Yā Qawiy 30 times*] *wasica kursiyyuhu's' samāwāti wal arḍi wa lā ya'uduhu ḥifẓuhumā, wa Huwa'l-cĀlīyyul cAẓīm.* [*Yā Qawiy* 26 times]

19. Bukhārī, *Kitāb al-Manāqib*, 1.

20. Bukhārī, *Kitāb al-Riqāq,* 38.

21. Bukhārī, *Kitāb al-Marḍā,* 3.

22. Haytamī, *Majmac al-Zawā'id*, 2/209, 10/146.

23. Ibn Māja, 2/1018.

24. Haytamī, *Majmac al-Zawā'id,* 9/24.

25. Ibn Māja, *Kitāb al-Zuhd*, 37.

26. Bukhārī, *Kitāb al-Riqāq*, 38.

27. This refers to the verse, *God erases what He will and confirms, and with Him is the Mother of the Book.* [13:39]

28. Bukhārī, *Kitāb al-Taḥajjud,* 14.

29. Bukhārī, *Kitāb al-Tawḥīd,* 50; Muslim, *Kitāb al-Dhikr*, 2,3.

30. Bukhārī, *Kitāb al-Shahādāt*, 16; Muslim, *Kitāb al-Zuhd*, 65, 66.

31. *Al-Futūḥāt al-Makkiyya* (*The Makkan Openings*); Best known work of Shaykh Muḥyuddīn ibn al-cArabī.

32. *Fuṣūṣ al-Ḥikam* (*The Chattels of Wisdom*); Highly esoteric work attributed to ibn cArabī.

33. *Al-Tā'iyya al-Kubrā*, the poem in *tā'*, also called *Naẓm al-Sulūk.* Ibn al-Fāriḍ, *Dīwān,* Beirut, 1953.

34. Such were Imāms al-Junayd, al-Jīlānī, al-Ghazalī, al-Suyūṭī, and latecomers such as ibn Idrīs and Abul-cAzāyem.

35. The reference to Sayyid cAlī al-cAydarūs seems to indicate that no man was nearer the Imām in both learning and spiritual stature than he, and this is why the Imām found solace only in his company.

36. *Riyāḍ al-Sālihīn*: *The Meadows of the Virtuous*. A famous collection of *ḥadiths* compiled by Imām al-Nawawī.

37. *ᶜAwārif al-Maᶜārif*: Seminal manual of Sufism by Shaykh Shihāb al-Dīn al-Suhrawardī.

38. Muḥammad Bā-Jubayr. A scholar who taught Imām al-Ḥaddād in his youth and became his disciple a few years later.

39. *Whomsoever We will, We raise in rank, and over everyone endowed with knowledge is one who knows better.* [12:76]

40. Abū Dāwūd, 3641; Tirmidhī, 2682.

41. *Risālat' al-Mudhākara*, published by the Starlatch Press as *The Book of Mutual Reminding*, Chicago, 2002.

42. *Risālat Ādāb Sulūk al-Murīd*, published by the Starlatch Press as *Good Manners of the Spiritual Disciple*, Chicago, 2002.

43. *Itḥāf al-Sā'il bi-Jawāb al-Masā'il*, published as *Gifts for the Seeker* by the Quilliam Press London, 1992.

44. *Al-Waṣāya al-Nāfiᶜa.*

45. *Al-Naṣā'iḥ al-Dīniyya wal-Waṣāyā al-Īmāniyya.*

46. *Risālat al-Muᶜāwana wal-Muẓāhara wal-Mu'āzara lil-Rāghibīn min al-Mu'minīn fī Sulūki Ṭarīqi'l-Ākhira,* published by the Quilliam Press, London, 1989, as *The Book of Assistance*.

47. *Sabīl al-Iddikār wal-Iᶜtibār bimā Yamurru bil-Insāni wa Yanqaḍī lahu min al-Aᶜmār,* published by the Quilliam Press, London, 1991, as *The Lives of Man*, reprinted by Fons Vitae, Louissville, KY.

48. *Al-Daᶜwa al-Tāmma wal-Tadhkira al-ᶜĀmma.*

49. *Al-Nafā'is al-ᶜUlwiyya fil-Masā'il al-Ṣūfiyya* to be published by the Starlatch Press as *The Sublime Treasures*.

50. *Al-Fuṣūl al-ᶜIllmiyya wal-Uṣūl al-Ḥikamiyya*, published by the Starlatch Press as *Knowledge and Wisdom*, Chicago, 2001.

51. The two great exponents of the orthodox theory of *Tawḥīd* for *sunni* Muslims are Ashᶜarī and Māturīdī. The first is followed by most followers of Imām Shāfiᶜī and Imām Mālik and the second by those of Imām Abū-Ḥanīfa. The differences between them are minor.

52. *Jāhid tushāhid*. Strive against your ego, when you conquer it you will contemplate the higher realities yourself, rather than hearing about them second hand.

53. *Key to the Garden* (*Miftāḥ al-Janna*) Arabic edition published in Cairo in 1969, reprinted in 1975, then again in Beirut in 1995 and 2000. English translation published by the Quilliam Press in 1990. The

passage in question constitutes its 17th chapter. See also *Gifts for the Seeker*, The Quilliam Press, 1992, pp. 11,12.

54. In one of his letters the Imām speaks of *ᶜĀlam al-Amr* thus: "It is the world of spirits which is too lofty and hidden to be either perceived with the senses or grasped by the rational mind. It is sufficient for the mind to believe in it and graciously accept whatever arrives from it."

55. *Kāf* and *Nūn* are the two letters that constitute the Divine command *Kun*! (Be!) that brings all things into existence.

56. The Zaydīs are the *Shīᶜa* of Northern Yemen, claiming to be followers of Imām Zayd, grandson of Imām Ḥusayn. They are much closer to the Sunnis than the Twelver *Shīᶜas* of Iran.

57. The cave of Thawr near Makka where they initially hid before emigrating to Madina. It was Abū Bakr's unrivalled privilege to accompany the Prophet may—God's blessings and peace be upon him—throughout his journey.

58. Shame in this world and the flames of Hell in the next.

59. Al-Ḥākim, *Mustadrak,* 1739.

60. The reference is to Mount Sinai where Moses, may peace be upon him, saw the Divine Manifestation upon the bush and, on more than one occasion, heard God speak to him.

A

Abdāl	Plural of *badal*; see *badal*.
Adab	Courtesy, good manners, the correct manner of doing something.
Ādāb	Plural of *adab.*
Ādhān	The call to each of the five obligatory ritual prayers.
Ahl	The people of….
Ahl-Allāh	The men of God.
Ahl-al-Bayt	The People of the House, the family of the Prophet, may God's blessings and peace be upon him and them.
Ahl-al-Aḥwāl	Those under the sway of a powerful spiritual state.
Ahl-al-Khaṭwa	The People of the Step. Those saints capable of crossing great distances by simply putting the right foot forwards and saying "*Bismillāh*" (In the Name of God).
Ahl-al-Sunna wal-jamāᶜa	The great majority of orthodox Muslims, as distinct from the Shīᶜa, *Muᶜtazilites*, and other minority sects.
Ahl al-Sirr	The people of the Secret. Those saints granted certain spiritual openings of a major nature.
Aqṭāb	Plural of *Quṭb*; see *Quṭb*.
Arwāḥ	Plural of *rūḥ*; see *rūḥ*.
Awliyā'	Plural of *walī*; see *walı*.
Awrād	Plural of *wird*; see *wird.*

ᶜA

ᶜĀlam A world, dimension, or level of existence, or a specific part thereof.

ᶜĀlam al-Amr The World of the Divine Command, sometimes taken to be synonymous with the World of the Spirits.

ᶜĀlam al-Arwāḥ The World of Spirits.

ᶜĀlam al-Mulk The physical world or world of dense forms. The lowest in the ternary *Mulk, Malakūt, Jabarūt.*

ᶜĀlam al-Nāsūt The human element in *ᶜĀlam al-Mulk.*

ᶜĀlam al-Shahāda The Visible World. Everything perceptible through the five senses. Corollary of *ᶜĀlam al-Ghayb,* which is the unseen.

ᶜĀlam al-Ṣuwar The World of Forms. Includes both the *Mulk* or World of Dense Forms and the *Malakūt* or World of Subtle Forms.

ᶜĀlam al-Ẓilāl The World of Shadows, which is the physical world seen as the dense shadows projected by higher realities. The expression is used to underline the illusory and ephemeral nature of the material level of existence.

ᶜĀlim Scholar, learned man.

ᶜĀrif One who knows. For Sufis: gnostic. He who knows by that direct spiritual perception which transcends sensory and mental knowledge. This is why they call him *ᶜĀrif bil-llah*, the one who knows by God, not by himself.

ᶜAṣr Late afternoon. An epoch. The mid-afternoon obligatory ritual prayer.

B

Badal A high-ranking member of the Circle of Sainthood by whose *du^{c}ā'* the Muslim community thrives and is protected from various calamities. Their number is forty according to some *ḥadiths*, and whenever one of them dies he is immediately replaced by another saint.

Basmalah The utterance: "*Bismillāh*", in the Name of God.

Baraka Benediction. Spiritual influence. The effect of the higher worlds on the material and psychic planes to cause things to thrive.

Barzakh That which separates. The intermediary world separating and connecting this world to the world of the resurrection. Also the intermediary world separating and connecting the material and spiritual dimensions.

D

Dā'ira Circle

Da^{c}wa Invitation. Summoning the people to answer the Divine call and accept God's invitation to Paradise and His presence.

Dīwān Collection of Sufi poems belonging to a single poet.

Dīwān al Awliyā The Conference of the Saints.

Dhikr To remember, or to mention. All kinds of teaching sessions of religious knowledge is called *Dhikr*. For Sufis; the remembrance of

God, whether using specific formulas or simply being aware of Him, whether silently or aloud, and whether alone or in congregation.

Du^ca' Calling upon. The word has come to retain only the religious meaning of prayer or supplication.

F

Faqīh One who understands well. Now used only to designate a jurisprudent, an expert in *sharī^ca*.

Farq Separation. For Sufis: *al-Farq al-Awwal*, the first separation, or the veiling of the servant from his Lord by his ordinary consciousness. *Al-Farq al-Thānī*, the second separation, is the return to ordinary consciousness after having achieved reunion and "arrived." Then, neither creation veils him from the Creator, nor the Creator from creation.

Fatḥ Opening, victory. *Fatḥ Makka*: The conquest of Makka. For Sufis: any grace received by the traveler to help him overcome the obstacles facing him. *Al-Fatḥ al-Kabīr*: The Major Opening which is the prerogative of the "elect of the elect" and leads to the unveiling of all the worlds, from the material to the Divine.

Fātiḥa The Opener. The opening *sūra* of the Qur'ān, the recitation of which is obligatory during every single *rak^ca* of the ritual prayer. It is also frequently recited to seal prayers and supplications and to be offered to the dead.

Fiṭra The pattern in which a thing was at its origin, at the beginning of its creation, before its modification by the action of time and the environment. The inborn qualities of a being. The primordial nature of mankind.

Futūḥ or *Futūḥāt* Plural of *Fatḥ*; e.g., *Futūḥ al-Ghayb*, *The Openings of the Unseen*, a book by Shaykh ^{c}Abdal-Qādir al-Jīlānī, and *al-Futūḥāt al-Makkiyya*, by Shaykh ibn al-^{c}Arabī.

G

Ghawth Succor. For the Sufis: The head of the hierarchy of saints, the supreme *Quṭb*.

Ghayba Absence. For Sufis: the spiritual state of being absent to creation when overwhelmed by the Divine Presence.

H

Ḥabīb Beloved. God's Greatest Beloved, *al-Ḥabīb al-A^{c}zam*, is one of the Prophet's names. *Al-Ḥabīb* came to be the title of the Ḥusaynī *sharīfs* of Ḥadramawt, the Ba-^{c}Alawī *sayyids*, from the 11th century of the *Hijra* onward.

Ḥadith Utterance, conversation. *Ḥadith Nabawī*, Prophetic utterance, the preserved traditions of the Prophet, may God's blessings and peace be upon him. *Ḥadith Qudsī*: Holy Tradition, the Divinity speaking on the tongue of the Prophet, may God's blessings and peace be upon him.

Ḥadra	Presence. For Sufis: the term on its own is used to designate a gathering of *dhikr*. The term qualified may mean the Divine Presence, *al-Ḥadra al-Ilāhiyya*, or the Prophet's presence, *al-Ḥadra al-Muḥammadiyya,* or any other presence.
Ḥajj	The greater Pilgrimage held yearly in the month of *Dhul-Ḥajja*. One of the five pillars of Islam, its various rites are symbols of the traveler's path to the Divine Presence.
Ḥalāl	Licit, lawful; as opposed to *ḥarām*.
Ḥaqīqa	Reality. The inner reality of things that can be perceived only by *kashf* or unveiling.
Ḥaqq	Truth. As a Divine Name it indicates He Who Alone truly is, He Who Alone is real..
Ḥaram	Sanctuary, sacred precinct. The two Noble Sanctuaries are Makka and Madina.
Ḥarām	Forbidden, illicit
Ḥawā	Passion, caprice, whim.
Ḥijr	The semicircular enclosure on the northern side of the Kaᶜba. It used to be part of the Kaᶜba in ancient days and is called *Ḥijr Ismāᶜīl*.
Hijra	Migration. The *Hijrī* calendar begins with the year of the Prophet's emigration from Makka to Madina.
Ḥizb	A party of people gathered for a special purpose. A political party. For Sufis: a collection of invocations strung together into a litany.
Himma	Resolution, determination, motivation.

I

^{c}Īd Feast. There are two main Muslim feasts: The greater one, *^{c}Īd al-Aḍḥā*, celebrating the completion of the *ḥajj*; and the lesser one, *^{c}Īd al-Fiṭr*, celebrating the completion of the fast of Ramaḍān.

Ilbās To cover or clothe with. For Sufis: the investiture with the *Khirqa*.

Iḥsān Thoroughness, excellence. The highest level of the triad mentioned in *ḥadith*: *Islām, Īmān, Iḥsān. Islām* corresponds to outward activity and therefore the physical world, the human body, and *sharī^{c}a*. *Īmān* corresponds to belief and emotional attachment to the tenets of faith, therefore to the subtle world, the human soul and *ṭarīqa*. *Iḥsān* corresponds to gnosis, therefore to the spiritual world of lights and *ḥaqīqa*.

Ijāza Permission, authority. The authorization granted by scholars to their students to teach a particular science. For Sufis, ^{c}Alawīs in particular: admission to the path, permission to recite certain *awrād,* or perform certain practices.

^{c}Ilm Knowledge, science.

^{c}Ilm ladunnī Inward knowledge of inspiration or unveiling.

Īmān Faith, belief; see *Iḥsān*

Imām Leader, leading authority.

Iqāma The second announcement for each of the five daily prayers. The first announcement, the *adhān*, calls people to the mosque, allowing them time to perform their *wuḍū'*. The second announcement or *iqāma* is made immediately before the *takbīr* heralding that the prayer has begun.

Irshād Guidance, counseling.

Ishā' The fifth ritual prayer of the day taking place approximately ninety minutes after sunset.

Islām To surrender or submit, see *Iḥsān*. Also the name divinely ascribed to all revealed religions, and therefore most suitable for the last revelation which embraces and completes all previous ones.

Ittiḥād Union. The union of two separate entities into a single new one. Sufis are accused by their detractors of claiming for themselves union with God. They reply that this is a logical impossibility since the Infinite cannot possibly unite with the finite and since God is not another "entity" to unite with. The technical term they use for union is *Jam*ᶜ which means that the finite may lose its own separative consciousness of itself and become conscious only of the Infinite. The finite does not thereby lose its existence by uniting with the Infinite, but only its ordinary consciousness of itself.

J

Jadhb Pull, attraction. For Sufis: the Divine pull that overpowers the seeker and takes him up to the Divine Presence, helping him overcome the downward pull of his earthy appetites and passions. It usually comes after he has achieved adequate preparation, rarely as pure grace without prior preparation.

Jam^{c} Union; see *Ittiḥād.*

Jawāz Permission, crossing over.

Jawāziyya The *khirqa jawāziyya* signifies the admission of the seeker as a traveler on the path, signaling thereby that he has crossed the boundary separating the stationary seekers of *baraka* from the actual travelers.

Jihād Struggle, battle. The Lesser *Jihād*, *al jihād al-asghar* is the military battle against infidel invaders. The Greater *Jihād*, *al jihād al-akbar*, is the spiritual struggle against the dark aspects of the soul to release it from its earthly shackles and allow it to soar up to its Lord. It is the Greater *Jihād* because it is a relentless struggle that allows for no rest and no distraction, whereas military *jihād* is confined to physical battlefields which are limited.

Jinn Beings made of the element fire and usually invisible to the physical eye. Some are Muslims and some not.

K

Karāma To honor, to treat with generosity. For Sufis: supernatural events wrought by saints, the miracles of saints, not Prophets. The extra-ordinary happenings *(Kharq al-^{c}āda)* by which God confirms, supports, and reassures the elect.

Karāmāt Plural of *karāma.*

Kashf Unveiling. For Sufis: the opening of the inward eye that perceives the subtle domain.

Khalīfa Deputy, successor. The *khalīfa* is the one who stands in for someone who is either absent (in which case he is deputy) or dead (in which case he is his successor.) In either case he must be qualified and invested with the power to shoulder his responsibility to the full. The position, or function, that the *khalīfa* occupies is called *al-khilāfa*. God's *khalīfa* on earth is firstly the supreme Pole, the head of the hierarchy of saints, and by extension all other saints who have attained to the supreme station in gnosis. The most precise term for *Khalīfa* would be vicar, were it not for its current connotations. The Prophet's *khalīfa* is his successor at the head of the Islamic state (Caliph) as long as he maintains himself within the boundaries of *sharī*ᶜ*a*. As for Sufi orders, the term *khalīfa* is used to designate either the master's deputy or his successor.

Khawārīj The heretic rebels who assassinated the third and fourth Rightly-Guided Caliphs. Their mark is that they apply the Qur'ānic verses condemning idolators and polytheists to the Muslims, denounce them as *kāfirs*, then have no qualms in killing them. Today's *khawārij* are those who believe that difference of opinion within the Muslim community is forbidden, that anyone who holds views different from their own is a *kāfir* and destined for Hell, and that they, although an absolute minority, are the only ones to go to paradise, whereas the remaining twelve billion Muslims are not Muslims at all.

Khirqa Small piece of cloth. For Sufis: whatever item of clothing a master may invest the disciple with.

Khilāfa Viceregency, succession; see *Khalīfa*

L

Labbayk The Muslim's answer when called, it means: "Yes! I am here listening and willing to obey."

M

Madad Reinforcement, supply. Reinforcing an army with men, increasing someone's wealth or children, and so on. For Sufis: reinforcing the traveler with assistance from the spiritual world.

Maghrib Sunset. The sunset obligatory ritual prayer.

Mahdī Rightly guided. The Leader promised to save the Muslims at the end of time when corruption and evil have reached their maximum. There are dozens of Prophetic traditions describing him and his function.

Maḥfūẓ Protected, guarded. The Guarded Tablet is *al-Lawḥ al-Maḥfūẓ*. Upon it the Divine Pen has inscribed all that is to happen from the beginning of creation to the Resurrection. It is guarded against interference and against unauthorized eyes.

Majdhūb One who is being pulled. For Sufis: an ecstatic; a man so powerfully attracted by the higher worlds that he loses his earthside consciousness or part thereof.

Malāmatī	A saint whose spiritual station is high but who shows no outward sign of it, his observable behaviour being ordinary. Although often confused with them, they are different from *ahl al-Takhrīb*, those who exhibit behavior that seemingly breaks the sacred law.
Malakūt	See *ᶜĀlam al-Malakūt*.
Maᶜrifa	Knowledge, information. For Sufis: gnosis, that knowledge that is directly perceived by the eye of the heart and which pertains to the Divine Acts, names and Attributes. In that respect it is higher than *kashf* or unveiling.
Mawlid	Birth. Prose or poetry compositions celebrating the Prophet's birth that are sometimes recited in gatherings that are themselves also called *mawlids*.
Miḥrāb	The prayer niche where the *Imām* stands to lead the ritual prayer in the mosque.
Minā	The valley between ᶜArafāt and Makka where the pilgrims camp for the three ᶜĪd days following the day of ᶜArafāt.
Miᶜrāj	Ladder, ascent. *Laylat' al-Mi'rāj* is the night the Prophet was taken up through the *Malakūt*, beyond the Throne, and into the Divine Presence.
Muazzin	The man who announces the five daily prayers by calling the *adhān* from the minaret.
*Mufassi*r	Qur'ānic exegete or commentator.
Muḥaḍara	God's imposed awareness of Him on Those whom He chooses, until such time that they are given the Opening.
Muḥaddith	Traditionist, expert on *ḥadith*.
Muᶜjiza	Miracle confirming Divine Messengers.

Mujaddid	Renewer.
Mujtahid	Striver, one who relies upon his own effort or *ijtihād*. In *sharī^{c}a*: an independent scholar capable of deriving the rulings of *sharī^{c}a* directly from the Qur'ān and *sunna*, rather than following any other authority such as the founder of any of the four schools of Islamic jurisprudence.
Mukāshafa	Unveiling; see *Kashf.*
Mulk	Kingdom; see *^{c}Ālam al-Mulk.*
Multazam	That portion of the wall of the Ka^{c}ba which is beneath its door and South of it over to the Black Stone. Pilgrims cling to it in the knowledge that this is one location where prayers are certain to be answered.
Munāfiq	Hypocrite.
Muqallid	Follower of a particular school of jurisprudence. A scholar who has not reached the stage of *ijtihād*. See also *mujtahid.*
Muqaddam	One who has been given prominence or leadership. *Al-Faqīh al-Muqaddam*: The Foremost Jurisprudent, title of Imām Muḥammad ibn ^{c}Alī Bā-^{c}Alawī. For certain Sufis, not for ^{c}Alawīs, the *muqaddam* is the *shaykh's* deputy.
Murīd	Aspirant, one who desires something. For Sufis: the seeker of truth, the disciple who aspires for gnosis.
Mushāhada	Contemplation. The direct vision of the Divine Names, Attributes and Acts. The real goal of the path.
Mutajarrid	One who has divested himself from all worldly possessions.

Mutaṣawwif One who has entered the Sufi path but not yet reached the stage of being a Sufi. A serious seeker as opposed to the *mustaṣwif* who imitates the Sufis outwardly with no serious intention of following their path.

Muzdalifa The valley separating ᶜArafāt from Minā. On leaving ᶜArafāt the pilgrims spend the night there or at least stop for a while before proceeding to Minā.

N

Nafs Soul, psyche, ego, self. The subtle form of a human being that is the transitional level between the luminous spirit and the dense body.

Naṣā'iḥ Plural of *naṣīḥa*; counsel.

Q

Qaḍā' Divine decree, the Divine decision in the preexisting Divine knowledge.

Qadar The execution of the decree in its predestined time and mode.

Qalb Heart.

Qawiy Strong, mighty.

Qaylūla The midday nap preceding the *Ẓuhr* prayer which was the Prophet's *sunna*.

Quṭb Pole, center of a circle, wheel, or sphere. For Sufis: the *Quṭb* is the supreme authority in each town, territory, or spiritual state. The Pole of Poles, *Quṭb al-Aqṭāb*, is *al-Ghawth*, the Succor.

R

Rābiṭa Bond.

Rajul Man. For Sufis: a man or woman true to their Adamic nature, having achieved the completion of virtue.

Rak^{c}a Unit of ritual prayer consisting in the recitation of the *Fātiḥa* and some others parts of the Qur'ān while standing, followed by one bow and two prostrations.

Ribāṭ Perseverance, continual performance of a function. To stand guard during wartime. To remain in a state of ritual purity in readiness for one ritual prayer after another. For ^{c}Alawīs the *ribāṭ* is a school for religious sciences.

Risāla Epistle, letter, treatise.

Riā' Ostentation, to perform a devotional act in public not for the sake of God but for other people's observation.

Riyāḍa Taming, training, disciplining.

Rubūbiyya Lordship.

Rūḥ Spirit.

S

Salām Peace. *Al-Salām* is a Divine Attribute. Greeting with the formula: *"Al-Salāmu ^{c}alaykum!"* (May peace be upon you!), which is the specifically Muslim way of greeting taught by the Prophet, may God's blessings (*salāt*) and peace (*salām*) be upon him.

Ṣalāt Prayer.

Salb Dispossession.

Sayyid — Master, lord. The term is used to designate the descendants of the Prophet through Imām Ḥasan or Imām Ḥusayn. The form *sayyiduna* means "our master."

Shādhilī — An affiliate of the Shādhilī Sufi order founded by Imām Abul-Ḥasan al-Shādhilī

Shafiʿī — A follower of the Shāfiʿī school of jurisprudence founded by Imām Muḥammad ibn Idrīs al-Shāfiʿī.

Shahāda — Witnessing, testimony; the two *shahādas* are *lā ilāha illa'llāh, Muḥammadun Rasūlu'llāh*; see also *ʿālam al-shahāda*.

Sharīʿa — Islamic sacred law.

Sharīf — Nobleman. A descendant of the Prophet.

Shaykh — Old man. For Sufis: the master of an order. For the various meanings of the word shaykh, see: *Key to the Garden* by *Ḥabīb* Aḥmad Mashhūr al-Ḥaddād, Starlatch Press, Chicago, 2003. pp. 136–137.

Shī'a — Heterodox Muslim minority who believe that the Caliphate belonged by right to Imām ʿAlī. There are two main sects of *shīʿa*: the Twelver *Shīʿas* of Iran and Iraq and the Zaydī *Shīʿa* of northern Yemen.

Ṣiddīq — Utterly veracious. For Sufis: the highest degree of sanctity.

Sirr — Secret. For Sufis: the Divinely bestowed special attribute or attributes that allow saints and spiritual masters to carry out their functions. Also: the highest element in the hierarchy comprising the body, soul, spirit and secret.

Sukr — Drunkenness, intoxication; see also *ghayba* and *jadhb*.

Sulūk — Traveling. A traveler is a *sālik.*

Sunna — Pattern of behaviour. In *sharī^{c}a*: the words and deeds of the Prophet, may God's blessings and peace be upon him.

Sunnī — One who belongs to *ahl al-sunna wal-jamā^{c}a*, i.e an orthodox Muslim. The term has been used abusively by fundamentalist groups who claim to be the true followers of the *sunna* and accuse the great majority of Muslims of overt heresy or even disbelief.

Sūra — A chapter of the Qur'ān of which there are one hundred and fourteen.

T

Tafsīr — Qur'ānic exegesis or commentary.

Tahkīm — Total authority. The old pattern of Sufism whereby the master required that the disciple surrender unconditionally to his authority. This method is unsuitable for today's disciples who have neither the power of certitude nor the spiritual resolution to sustain such training.

Tā'iyya — Poem in *tā'*.

Talwīn — Changing colour. For Sufis: the changes that appear on the traveler under the influence of successive states.

Tamkīn — Mastery, firm establishment. No changes appear on the master who dominates his spiritual states rather than being dominated by them.

Taqwā — The fear of God. To act in the constant awareness of His Presence.

Ṭarīqa — A particular way or method of doing something. For Sufis: the technique, whether outward or inward, particular to each order. By extension, the order itself.

Tawḥīd — Unification. *Shahādat'al-tawḥīd*: the Testimony of Divine Unity, *lā ilāha illa'llāh*. Unification is to acknowledge only one Divinity and to unify all one's abilities and emotions into the single-minded pursuit of nearness to that Divinity.

U

ᶜUbūda — This is a term coined by the Sufis to designate the state of total slavehood. It is the highest degree in the triad: *ᶜIbāda* or worshiping God. *ᶜUbūdiyya*: being a through and through servant of God inwardly by remaining serene and content throughout whatever tests or hardships He has chosen to impose and by renouncing desire for anything that differs from His will. *ᶜUbūda*: having no will other than that of God."

ᶜUbūdiyya — Servitude; see above.

Uns — Intimate satisfaction, inward comfort. For Sufis: a spiritual state brought about by the unveiling of the Divine Attributes of Beauty, which makes it the expansive corollary of the contraction brought about by the unveiling of the Divine Attributes of Majesty and termed *Hayba*, awe.

W

Walī	Protégé, ally, close friend, supporter, also governor, caretaker. "*God is the Walī of those who believe,*" says the Qur'ān [2:257]. All believers are *awliyā'* in the general acceptance of the term since they have chosen God for their protector and ally. For Sufis: a *walī* is he whom God has taken under his special protection and enveloped in his solicitude, eventually to elevate him into His Presence.
*Wara*ᶜ	Scrupulousness.
Wilāya	The attribute of the *walī*.
Wird	A regular devotional function.
Wuḍū'	Ritual ablutions.

Y

Ya-Sīn	The thirty sixth *sūra* of the Qur'ān said by the Prophet to be the "heart of the Qur'ān." Also one of the Prophet's names.

Z

Zakāt	The obligatory tax paid yearly as an act of worship by any Muslim possessing over a *niṣāb* or minimum requirement in money, crops, cattle, or commercial goods. It is one of the five pillars of Islam.
Zaydī	The *Shī*ᶜ*a* sect of Northen Yemen who claim to have originated with Imam Zayd, grandson of Imām Ḥusayn.
Ẓuhr	Noon; the midday ritual prayer.